UNDERSTANDING EVERYDAY GOVERNMENTS' WAYS OF JOB CREATION

UNDERSTANDING EVERYDAY GOVERNMENTS' WAYS OF JOB CREATION

Ideas and Governments' Sustainable Strategy to Facilitate
Success in Job Creation

André Hakizimana

iUniverse, Inc.
Bloomington

Understanding Everyday Governments' Ways of Job Creation
Ideas and Governments' Sustainable Strategy to Facilitate Success in Job Creation

iUniverse books may be ordered through booksellers or by contacting:

iUniverse
1663 Liberty Drive
Bloomington, IN 47403
www.iuniverse.com
1-800-Authors (1-800-288-4677)

ISBN: 978-1-4759-6404-2 (sc)
ISBN: 978-1-4759-6405-9 (ebk)

Library of Congress Control Number: 2012922316

Printed in the United States of America

iUniverse rev. date: 1/04/2013

To my colleagues and my professors in economics

CONTENTS

▼

AUTHOR'S NOTE

▼

Environment for Job Creation:
Ideas and Successes

Since 2007, and especially from the beginning of the 2008 financial crisis in Europe and North America, we have heard shouts:

> "I've been out of work since 2008, and I have no hope of finding a job."
> "Our company closed down yesterday, and my job will end tomorrow."
> "There are job cuts, and I can't find a job."
> "I sent twenty copies of my CV where I thought I could find a job, but I've received no responses."
> "All jobs advertised need work experience, but I have none."
> "I am in a catch-22 situation."
> "I graduated three years ago and still don't have a good job."

Political parties and governments are engaged in debates to facilitate job creation; so far it appears that there is no tangible solution for sustainable job creation. Every day I hear that financial institutions, private companies, and public sectors are closing down.

To create a successful environment for job creation, our governments need to implement sustainable economic policies. We have no hope of finding jobs because the governments are not devising economic strategies for sustaining employment. Instead of new ways to sustain employment, they always use same policies that have been used, and those policies have already failed to maintain an increase in employment.

We need the governments who are creative in practical ways to facilitate job creation, because the old ways of job creation cannot face today's economic challenges. Can we ordinary people create an environment for job creation? We can, but we need to understand the everyday strategy for job creation in order to be able to contribute in the debate of political parties and governments with which we are affiliated. We need debates that result in sustainable strategies to facilitate sustainable job creation. In this context, instead of political parties blaming each other, they need to create favourable environment dedicated to sustain a rise in employment.

Do we undestand the position of political parties in relation to job creation during their election campaigns and debates? During elections we vote for political parties with which we're affiliated, or that we believe can fulfil our needs. After elections, do we get the results for which we voted? If not, how do we use our vote in the next election, in order to get the results we want? Do we understand politicians' ideas during their election campaign?

This book attempts to explain the concepts politicians use in their election campaigns and debates, but the ambition of this book is to point out practical ways for sustainable job creation. Moreover, it identifies the everyday principles of economics to increase and sustain employment. This book identifies all practical ways and ideologies used since the Great Depression to create growth in Europe and North America. It embodies past experiences of job creation and the strategy of job creation. I assume if you are reading this book, your ambition is to change the status quo. I'm sure that if we all know the everyday economic strategy, then together we can create an unshakable environment which can sustain growth.

The Role of Government

The role of government is to provide incentives to businesses. In this context, the government needs to develop infrastructures such as information and communication technology, and occasionally businesses need grant relief and subsidies from the government.

Moreover, the role of government is education and maintaining the security of its country against aggression from external sources, as well as securing the standard of living of its citizens. The government uses taxes for maintaining all country services. In general, a government provides goods and services that cannot be provided by businesses or other private sectors. In addition, it create an environment that is able to sustain the profitability of businesses.

Free Market Concept

The free market concept originated in the late eighteenth century and was introduced by Adam Smith, in his proposal of classical economic theory in contrast to the mercantile theory of trade and policy that had prevailed in the United Kingdom.[1] The basic concept of mercantile theory was the belief that national wealth is measured by the amount of gold and silver a country possesses. In addition, although government regulation of foreign trade was a key for ensuring the country's wealth and the security of the state, the mercantile theory held that colonies exist for the economy of the colonialist. The mercantile theory focuses on regulation of trade, whereas classical economic theory focuses on free trade, and thus free markets and free competion in trade. Therefore, in classical economic theory individuals have a right to what they can gain for themselves on the labour markets. In other words, in free markets, individuals are free to sell their labour to survive. If an individual is unable to sell his or her labour in his or her country, then he or she has right to migrate to another country to sell labour in order to survive.

In this context, businesses have a right to put their plants and factories in any country or areas where their capital costs are lower. Thus businesses put their plants where they can gain more profit. At this point, the restriction of the government to exclude trading rights to businesses opposes the principles of free markets. In free markets, economies work better without government intervention in any way, and individuals follow their fate. Furthermore, in free markets there is no need to bail

---

[1] See Adam Smith (1776), *An Inquiry into the Nature and Cause of the Wealth of Nations.*

out businesses because the businesses can fix their financial problems themselves.

However, as we know, all developed countries failed to adhere to these principles of free markets, and in the future their adherance is also in question because of the natural rates of unemployment and businesses' reliance on government subside.

Capitalism

According to the *Oxford English Dictionary* (Vol 2, p. 863), the word *capitalism* was first used in English by William Makepeace Thackeray in 1854, in his novel *The Newcomes* (1855, Vol 2, p. 45). In this context the word *capitalist* was first used in English in the 1780s by Arthur Young (*Travels in France*), and it was used by Turgot in his *Reflections on the Formation and Distribution of Riches* (LXIII-IV, 1770).

Many politicians' explaination of capitalism is somehow interpreted as free markets. However, capitalism is a society that is founded on institutions that favour and respect individuals' freedoms and the right of choice of their fate. The right of individuals include the right to work, trade, and education, as well as the standard of living. Capitalistic society replaced Feudalism society, which was founded on institutions that were contrary to individual belief.

Welfare States

In the political arena, some politicians are against government policies regarding welfare states; they argue that the regulation of the welfare state inhibits the incentive of business because key policies of the welfare states are to protect and sustain economy based on social well-being. Moreover, the principles of social welfare states are equality of opportunity, equitable distribution of wealth, and helping those unable to sell their labour. In this context, welfare states introduced a social welfare programme which sustains the unemployed. This programme is available in Western countries; however, it is provided on the basis of different principles for each country. In this respect, social welfare programmes provide health insurance, retirement benefits, and jobseeker allowance to people unemployed, as well as benefiting people with disabilities. Western countries can be identified as welfare states because they protect populations from life's insecurities.

Supply Side Economics

In general, supply side economics focuses on tax, regulatory, and monetary policies in order to increase employment. Monetary policy is concerned with maintaining actions such as increasing interest rates and supplying money in the markets. In other words, supply side economics focuses on low cost to increase the willingness of producers to create more goods and services. Many economists would agree that supply side economics is a better way to recover the economy in contrast to Keynesian economists, who recommend more government spending, Supply side economists recommend a reduction in government spending, deregulation, and tax cuts.

Laffer explained these strategies.[2] He argues that reductions in federal taxes on the businesses, and a reduction on the individual income, would lead to economic growth. President Ronald Reagan implemented the concept in the 1980s, and Laffer's strategies boosted US economic growth.

Keynesian Economics[3]

Keynesian economics focuses on how government spending can sustain employment. Although many economists argue that cutting wages can restore full employment, Keynes argues that businesses cannot employ people in order to produce goods and services that cannot

---

[2] See the Laffer Center, "Supply-Side Economics", available online from http://www.laffercenter.com/supply-side-economics.

[3] See Keynes (1935), *The General Theory of Employment, Interest and Money.*

be sold. Therefore his economics considers government spending in order to stimulate economy. In this context, if the government increases spending in education or subsidises businesses, then employment can resume. In this respect, government tax breaks to both businesses' and households' income would boost economy.

During economic downturn, it is necessary to cut wages which were increased during economic growth. However, employment would only resume because of a rise in consumption.

Government Spending

To resolve the problem of government spending is to create an environment that maintains employment. For example, work placement of both university graduates and youth are needed, otherwise government expenditures will continue to rise. Because of an increase in transfer payments to pension schemes and other services, there is little that can be done to limit government spending. Only young employment can offset a rise in the government expenditures.

Government Budget Deficit

Government budget deficit occurs when the government spends more money than it has coming in. A decrease in the government taxes revenue is caused by a fall in employment. Moreover, government budget deficit is caused by lack of the government's vision of country resources for economic output. In this context, the lack of vision causes a misallocation of its spending. When a government increases its spending in the wrong investment, it decreases the country's gross domestic products (GDP), which in turn negatively affects its budget. The solution to the budget deficit is to create sustainable jobs, and the government needs to spend its resources in the country for economic output.

Austerity

In general, austerity refers to the measures taken by a government to reduce its spending in order to reduce government budget deficit. Thus, austerity measures decrease the services and benefits provided by government. In this respect, moreover, government deficit can be reduced by raising taxes. Furthermore, the government borrows money to finance its deficit; however, interest rates must be paid on money borrowed. In this way, government deficit will continue to rise if the economy continues to decline. An austere budget is about reducing government deficit, not creating jobs.

INTRODUCTION

▼

Debates on Practical Ways to Facilitate Job Creation

Since the 2008 international economic crisis, much of the debate about job creation has been confined to government spending and austerity. Some argue that government spending plays an important role in job creation and in economic recovery; others argue that only austerity plays a crucial role. This book is designed for readers interested in the current debate on how Western governments influence job creation. Moreover, it explains a theory underlying how to influence job creation. The book also explains political party convictions and their arguments to facilitate jobs creation. Furthermore, it incorporates the suggestion of what the Eurozone governments can do to influence job creation. The content of this book is clearly explained, providing the reader scenarios that can be used by governments to either boost or facilitate job creation.

The ambition of this book is also designed for the reader interested in policy debate on employment, and it addresses the way businesses increase profits. The book is not designed for only the reader interested in the current policy debate on employment—it is also designed for the businesses who wish to increase more knowledge of how to make more profit.

First the book is oriented towards the role of both government spending and austere budget in job creation. It focuses on understanding how government spending or austere budget contributes to job creation. In other words, what are the ways the government can strongly affect economic recovery and sustain employment?

Second, it recognizes the importance of both government expenditures and austerity measures. An austere government budget is necessary when the country's budget is in deficit—but it is the opposite towards job creation. The book also makes suggestions for what is needed to sustain job creation during both economic growth and recession.

Third, the book focuses on the motives that can cause businesses to create more jobs. Fourth, it explores the arguments of the Conservative Party and the Social Democratic Party in relation to job creation.

Fifth, the book reviews the origins of the European Union and the policy development it pursued in relation to the creation of jobs, as well as the main reason that pushed Eurozone leaders to introduce the European Fiscal Treaty.

The book reviews the European Union policy for economic integration and for job creation, particularly how European Union resolves the problem of university graduates and youth unemployment. Moreover, this book identifies all practical ways used since 1929 to create and sustain economic growth in the United States of America.

Organisation

This book is organized into six chapters. Chapter one focuses on government spending and the reduction of budget. It examines both how government spending and austerity policies can create jobs. Though the book addresses the road taken by Ireland's government to recover its economy, it suggests pragmatic ways to create sustainable jobs. The book discusses the various types of markets failures, and it investigates the origins of past recessions. Can policy makers prevent recession? The response is in this chapter regarding the way government can bring back confidence in the markets during recession.

In chapter two the book focuses on businesses and their motivation to create more jobs. It also explores possible ways the government can boost employment in the small- and medium-sized enterprises.

Chapter three introduces the reader to the origin of political party ideology. It examines the party differences in relation to job creation, and it discusses fundamental consideration of political parties in relation to taxation, budget deficit reduction, and regulation. Although during election campaigns, political parties many understand what they intend to accomplish, this chapter clearly indicates how political parties are limited by their ideology, discussing the integrity of political parties in relation to their choices on how to build a country.

Chapters four and five focus on the European Union, discussing its origin and goals. It investigates the early developments of the European Union and its policy developments to tackle unemployment. The Fiscal Treaty is introduced in chapter four. What motivated Germany and France to introduce the Fiscal Treaty in the European Union Treaty? Additionally, the book examines the importance of economic integration. Can Eurozone and European Union become a strong, integrated economy? What more is needed in the Eurozone economic integration? How can Eurozone resolve the problem of university graduates and youth unemployment? Chapters four and five view the possibilities to answer these fundamental questions. This book suggests what the European Union and Eurozone governments can do to influence more job creation. In fact, tough rules are needed in the European Union economic integration, and more regulations in the Eurozone services are a prerequisite in order to sustain the Eurozone economy.

How do governments create and sustain growth? Chapter six identifies all practical ways used since 1929 to create and to sustain growth in the Unites States of America. It determines that early government intervention is imperative for rescuing the economy when the country is in financial failure. Moreover, it identifies that America's domestic demand is not enough to sustain its economy. The United States' exports are a key principal for the its economic growth.

CHAPTER I

▼

Government Spending versus Austerity

1. Government Spending

There's no doubt that government spending has the potential to improve market efficiency when market failures occur. Thus, government spending can create jobs. In this respect, when there are market failures, government spending has the potential to create jobs by moving away from markets' failures produced by deregulation. Moreover, although government spending is likely to reduce the creation of jobs when markets function perfectly, it is necessary to know the meaning of market failures to be able to understand when government spending is critical for job creation.

The meaning of a market failure is not poverty, social inequality, fraud and corruption, high prices, and a bankruptcy—these are a result of governments' policy inefficiency in economic strategy. The meaning of a market failure is identified as an imperfect market; that is, a market without competitiveness. In other words, imperfect markets are unproductive markets. Instead of engaging in productivity which reduces cost of goods and services, imperfect markets increase prices of goods and services. Furthermore, imperfect markets can drive prices below cost. In this context, economic theory has identified the types of market failures:

a. Monopolistic Markets

The supposition that competitive markets lead to efficient markets is because producers or sellers do not have the market power to impose prices or costs on other markets. However, monopolistic markets can impose prices in order to gain high profits. In this context, an increase in prices in a monopolistic market would trigger inflation in markets, which in turn would cause market failure. In this regard, although housing markets are not considered monopolistic markets—because housing markets are planned and driven by the government—they can be identified as a government monopolistic market. Governments have power in the housing market because they control housing land. A government has the power to impose how many houses can be built through land zoning. The result of the increase of housing construction is a rise in the prices of house. Thus, a rise in the house price is caused by an increase in the house construction. At this stage only the government can stop an increase in the price of houses. The housing market is a market failure.

b. Public Goods

In general, the government provides public goods. Although there is a rivalry and thus competitiveness in the consumption of private goods, there is non-rivalry in public goods. Public goods are excluded in competitive markets. Moreover, public goods are unproductive because they are both financed and purchased by government. An example of a public good is national defence. When a government increases its expenditures in the army, it could cause market failures. For example, since 2003 the American government has increased its expenditures in funding the army; this not only caused the American economy to slow down in 2008, but it also caused the American economy to take longer to recover. When the American army came home from the Iraq war at the end of 2011, the American economy started showing a strong sign of recovery. Thus the American economics indicated a green shoot for recovery because the government reduced its expenditures in the Iraq war.

c. Externalities

In the market, some goods create externalities[4] in their consumption or production. But externalities can be either positive or negative. Pollution is an example of a negative production externality, because it causes a whole society to bear the cost of environment degradation. In this context, a factory may discharge pollution into a river, reducing fish stocks downstream and making river water unsuitable for use. At this point, because the producer does not pay the cost of the pollution, the price of goods is lower. As a result, this leads to inefficient overproduction and overconsumption of the goods. In this regard, if goods generate a negative externality because of overproduction and overconsumption, it does not mean that markets should stop producing these goods. The goods should be produced, but consumption should be reduced to a level where the negative externality does not cost society.

A vaccine represents an example of positive externality. When a person is vaccinated against communicable or transmissible disease, society benefits because that person cannot spread the disease to others.

d. Lack of Perfect Information

Free markets work efficiently when both sellers and buyers are informed. If the seller is more informed than the buyers, the market result is inefficient. For example, in insurance markets, buyers of insurance know more about their riskiness than sellers. As a result, only buyers with higher risks will tend to purchase more insurance, because they are certain that the benefit of the insurance will exceed the cost. This strategy causes an increase in the prices of insurance. In this context, the lenders may not have incentives for taking risks compared to the borrowers.

In the above discussion, government spending can create jobs when markets fail. Thus in terms of job creation, governments can increase their expenditures when markets fail. However, in the absence of

---

4   An externality is an economic cost.

market failures, government spending depresses investment because it increases both inflation and interest rates in the market, which itself slows down economic growth.

Government expenditures can create jobs through three ways. One way is through social sectors spending. The second way is through the production of services such as education, infrastructure, information and communications technology, and health. Finally, government can create jobs by lowering taxation in the business, because low tax increases profits in businesses, which in turn stimulates growth. In addition, the government needs to invest more in productive sectors than in unproductive sectors. The table indicates sectors which are productive and unproductive.

Table 1

Government Unproductive Sectors	Government Productive Sectors
• Social Security • Social Welfare • Social Housing • Defence • Community Amenities • Recreational Cultural	• Public Services • Education • Health • Infrastructure • Transportation • Communication • Research and Development

Government expenditures in unproductive sectors are needed to reduce social inequality and to facilitate the social inclusion of those with less income and the recipients of social welfare. Unproductive sectors contribute to job creation by increasing consumption, which in turn increases demand. An increase in the demand of goods and services is a source of economic recovery. Although social security payments and other transfer payments may reduce private saving rates by replacing the private saving for retirement, recipients of social welfare and pensioners use their income to buy goods and services from both the public and private sectors.

Government expenditures in productive sectors maintain growth. Among the productive sectors is education. Education is productive because it sustains both productivity and innovation. In this context, government spending in education improves human capital; thus education plays an important role in human skills and expertise at the workplace. In this respect, the contribution of the human capital to the economy includes its effect on production and its effect as sources of technology innovation.

Expenditure in health is also productive because good health sustains the capability of the human being in the labour force. For example, good health in childhood reduces school absenteeism and early drop-out rates. Moreover, children with better health can be expected to attain higher educational levels and therefore be more productive in the future. In contrast, poor health negatively affects productivity and increases social inequality, because poor health can cause low earnings, which in turn cause a rise in the government expenditures. Only good health can enhance the likelihood of participation in the education and labour forces, which itself causes high earnings, and high earnings create more jobs than low earnings because workers with high earnings spend more while, increasing their savings (which also boosts employment). The performance of the health sector can positively reduce government expenditures in health while contributing to an increase in the stock of human capital, itself sustains economic growth. At this stage, government expenditures in education and health can stimulate economic growth over the medium-term and long-term, if it has been planned in advance.

In this context, in addition to education and good health, a long-term growth rate is sustained only by the population growth and the rates of technical change, which is explained by externality. At this point, however, a negative externality such as pollution would increase the cost of environment degradation. As discussed earlier, although the negative externality would downgrade economic growth, a positive externality such as vaccines would increase the likelihood of good health in society. In this context, in the absence of government spending on vaccines, vaccines would be both under-produced and under-consumed. So the government spending in health increases the likelihood of good health in people's lives while maintain job creation, because vaccines are periodically consumed.

Infrastructure contributes to job creation through direct investment, and good infrastructures facilitate productivity in the private sector as well as improving health and education. For example, access to clean water and sanitation improves health while reducing the cost of boiling water, thus reducing electricity bills. In this regard, the government's current spending on the maintenance of roads, health, and schools infrastructures is vital because it is maintaining the quality of the services of both public services and private services while maintaining productivity in these services.

Governments should consider spending on public services in order to improve both performance and productivity at the workplace. For example, government enforcement of property rights may lead to more entrepreneurial activity and also may reduce the costs of supplying private-sector goods to markets. In this respect, reducing government expenditure can lower private sector productivity because without government enforcement, this could increase costs in supplying goods to markets.

In general, government expenditures are necessary for creating jobs and sustaining employment. Government spending needs only to be directed in markets that are unable to improve. In this regard, however, unplanned government spending would have less effect on market failure. If government spending is considered to replace private investment, this would cause a decrease in the private investment—which in turn would cause a decrease in the government revenue. In other words, the dangers of excessive government expenditures depress private investment while increasing government deficit, which itself further depresses the lenders of markets.

2.   Can Austerity Cause Economic Recovery?

Although past information could not necessarily be referenced to understanding whether austerity can cause economic recovery or create jobs, exploring both past recession and strategies used for economic recovery can help to answer the above question.

In the United States, the 1929-1933 recession, also known as the Great Depression, was caused by high inflation rates that prompted an increase rate of the Federal Reserve Fund from 1928 to 1929. In this way, because high interest rates limited liquidity in the hand of consumers and investors, the increase in the rate triggered the stock market crash in 1929. This crash was followed by the move to sell dollars for gold. Subsequently, an increase in the sales of dollars caused the dollar to appreciate. At this stage, the Federal Reserve raised interest rates to tighten the dollars in circulation, and this caused bankruptcies; thus, 9,755 commercial banks in the United States ceased operation (Labonte and Makinen, 2002). In this context, despite the link of the United States with other countries through exchange rates embodied in the gold standard, which limited the Federal Reserve to prevent high inflation, the Great Depression was aggravated by the Federal Reserve tightening the dollar in circulation in the United States. Thus the long-lasting recession of 1929-1933 was caused by tight monetary policy in United States, which provoked the stock market crash.

It is not only the recession of the 1929-1933 that originated from high inflation rates; the recession of 1937-1938 also originated from an increase in inflation, which urged the Federal Reserve to tighten its monetary policies. In addition to tightening monetary policy, the government increased fiscal measures in early 1937, which included tax increases. The government reversed these measures in early 1938 because of the trough of the recession. At this period, the origin of high inflation was the New Deal, policies of social and economic reform that President Franklin D. Roosevelt introduced in the 1930s. The New Deal increased the federal government expansion through debt, growing from 16 per cent of gross domestic product in 1929 to 40 per cent in 1936 (Velde, 2009). Despite the depreciation of the dollar in 1934, there was increasing inflation as a result of an increase in political instability in Europe, which encouraged long-term capital flows in the United States.

Furthermore, the 1969-1970 recession was preceded by a period of inefficient investments, which caused unstable growth that led to increased inflation. Inflation rose from 3.1 per cent in 1967 to 4.3 per cent in 1968, 4.9 per cent in 1969, and 5.3 per cent in 1970. Many contemporary observers attributed this boom-and-bust pattern to the fiscal policy stance of the time, arguing that the easing of fiscal policy was prompted by American military involvement in the Vietnam War, and the government was unwilling to raise taxes to finance the war. To reduce inflation, the federal funds rate was increased from about 5 per cent in March 1968 to 9 per cent in August 1969. Additionally, the government made efforts to reduce the budget deficit, which reduced aggregate spending. There were also a 10 per cent tax increase to individual income and corporate tax. Moreover, the government passed the Tax Reform Act of 1969, whose main provisions were the repeal of the investment tax credit and the restriction of the tax-exempt status of foundations (Velde, 2009). Thereafter, in addition to easing fiscal measures, the reduction in the federal funds rate was lowered from 9 per cent to 3 per cent. As a result, the easing of fiscal measures and monetary policies helped economic growth in 1970.

The decision to relatively ease fiscal measures and monetary policies caused the recession to end, but these measures were a result of the continuing high inflation rate. Even though there was a rise in oil prices between 1973 and 1975, there was again a rise in the inflation, and again the government applied a monetary policy to reduce an increase in the inflation rate. The federal funds rate increased from 5 per cent in late in 1972 to 10 per cent in mid-1973. Moreover, there was a cut in federal government expenditure in 1974, which caused the 1973-1975 recession. This recession was a long and deep recession that is remembered primarily for its simultaneous rise in both the inflation rate and the unemployment rate (Labonte and Makinen, 2008). Many countries—including Ireland, the United Kingdom, France, Japan, and West Germany—experienced the 1973-1975 recession. In the United States, when the tax reduction passed in 1975, there was again a resumption of federal government spending, which was estimated to lower revenue by 1.4 per cent of GDP in 1975. The act's provisions were a tax rebate, which was sent out in the second quarter of 1975. The act also expanded individual income tax credits, increased the investment tax credit, and reduced corporate tax rate (see CRS Report 92-90E). This act helped economic recovery; however, the economic recovery was followed by the "double dip" recession of the 1980s, caused by the desire of the federal reserve to reduce the inflation rate, which reached 11.1 per cent on an annualised basis in the fourth quarter of 1980.

This rise in the inflation rates was probably a result of the revolution in Iran, which made the price of oil rise from thirteen dollars per barrel at the beginning of 1979 to thirty-seven dollars per barrel in March 1981 (Labonte and Makinen, 2008). To reduce this inflation rate, the Federal Reserve increased federal funds rate from approximately 10.5 per cent in August 1979 to 17.5 per cent in April 1980. The federal funds rate was lowered until it reached about 9.5 per cent in August 1980. However, because the high inflation rate remained stubborn, a further round of rate increase brought it to 19 per cent in July 1981. In this respect, the federal funds rate remained above 10 per cent until the second recession had ended, in October 1982 (Labonte and Makinen, 2008).

In addition to the major provisions of the Economic Recovery Tax Act of 1981, which included reductions in marginal income tax rates and individual saving incentives, the large tax cuts in 1981 played a role in stimulating the economy in 1982 (Labonte and Makinen, 2008). Some other countries experienced the 1980s recession, like Ireland and the United Kingdom. The recession of 1990-1991 was not long, lasting for three-quarters of a year (Labonte and Makinen, 2008). The cause of this recession was that the Federal Reserve raised the federal funds rate between February 1988 and May 1989 from around 6.5 per cent to 9 per cent. Another cause was Iraq's invasion of Kuwait, which caused crude oil to rise from a previous average of fifteen dollars per barrel to thirty-three dollars a barrel in June 1990. Moreover, some analysts believed that the uncertainty surrounding the crisis also played a significant role in undermining business and consumer confidence, and this in turn led to the curtailment of aggregated spending until the crisis resolved (Labonte and Makinen, 2008). Like the recessions discussed above, the 1990s recession ended because of policies involving monetary easing, lowering interest rates, and declining oil prices.

Recessions can originate from high inflation rates, but the recessions of 1953-1954 and 1957-1958 were caused by a falling gross domestic product. These two recessions were marked by a significant increase in unemployment rate. From February to October in 1945, there was a decline in government spending at the end of World War II, and this decline led to a huge drop in GDP. Moreover, after the Korean War in 1954, the Federal Reserve restricted the circulation of the dollar because of a fear of inflation. Thus both fiscal measures and over-tightening of monetary policy in 1953-1954 and 1957-1958 caused the decline in GDP. Before the recession began, President Truman called for a significant expansion in government spending through a series of new programs (the Fair Deal) that were to be financed through an increase in taxes. Therefore, in addition to both tax cuts, increased spending was applied in the 1948 and 1949 to offset revenue reductions; an easing policy followed in the mid-1960s.

Although the above clarifications specified that the origin of recessions are from government expansionary policy, such as an increase in the government expenditure or lowering interest rates and vice versa, the 2001 recession was caused by a decline in investments, in Internet firms. Thus, even though the September 2001 terrorist attack played an important role in undermining public confidence in spending and investing, the collapse of the dot-com bubble occurred between 1995 and 2001 and was the origin of the 2001 recession (see also L. Kliesen, 2003). Despite the fact that there was a growth in computer and software in 1999, computer and software sales were the main contributors of the decline of industrial production. Moreover, the decline in industrial production caused a decline in real net exports in 2001. Real exports of goods and services fell about 10 per cent, and the largest percentages were generally for exports destined in Asia: South Korean at -58.4 per cent, Taiwan at -37.3 per cent, and Japan at -37.0 per cent (see Kliesen, 2003). By contrast, the housing market continued to grow.

As discussed above, to recover the American economy, the Federal Reserve responded by easing monetary policy, or decreasing interests rates, while the government increased expenditure. In this way, the Federal Reserve lowered the federal funds rate between January 3 and December 11, 2001: the rate was reduced from 6.5 per cent to 1.75

per cent (Labonte and Makinen, 2008). Moreover, tax rebates and the reduction in personal income tax rates were used to increase households' consumption. However, despite these policy responses, the housing market stimulated economic growth because it was not affected by the 2001 recession. Therefore it is hard to think that economic recovery in this period was caused by lowering interest rates or government spending.

In Ireland, the 2008 recession stemmed from excessive loans to developers and to borrowers from the middle class. The recession in the United States was caused by issuing mortgages to subprime borrowers—that is, mortgages made to those who are in a category considered to be relatively at high risk: people with a lesser ability to repay the loan based on personal criteria. Therefore, in 2006-2007 interest rates began to rise, and housing prices started to drop; consequently, prices failed to go up as anticipated by the investors, and in many part of United States, refinancing became more difficult. Moreover, foreclosure activities increased dramatically, and adjustable rates mortgages (ARM) interest rates were reset higher. By the end of 2006, accelerated foreclosures soared in United States. The effect of this crisis was a worldwide financial crisis throughout 2007 and 2008. In this way, the breakdown of three of the largest US investment banks—Lehman Brothers, Bear Stearns, and Merrill Lynch—augmented the instability in the United States financial system.

In summary, in addition to market failures, the origin of recession is an increase in government expenditures, high inflation rates, and a rise of interest rates as well as tax increase. Moreover, recessions are a result of inefficiencies of the country's investments; that is, excessive investments directed in a single market sector, such as the housing market. When policymakers channel excessive investments in a single market sector, the sector becomes the only engine of the country's economy that can create jobs. Therefore declines in the demand in this sector will cause sluggish GDP and slow the creation of jobs. For example, the 2008 debts crisis in the United States and Ireland originated from excessive credit channelled into the housing market. As a consequence, the decline in house selling caused the recession in both countries' economies. At this stage, because of the incapability of policymakers to increase the purchasing power of consumers, many argue that an increase in government expenditure and lowering interest rates could be strong responses to the recessions.

However, the 2001 recession elucidated that government spending is a weak response to the recessions. Thus, instead of expansionary, the recovery of the 2001 recession in United States was caused by easing loans in the housing markets, which had continued to grow from the 1990s. It was the growth in investments in the housing market that created a boom—which busted in 2008 and caused the current debts crisis. In this respect, the response to the recessions is timely to natural market recovery, not on policy response. In other words, the response to the recession is timely on the market's investments opportunity. Policy expansion plays an important role in relation to innovation so that its response to the recession could become positive after many years. On the other hand, some argue that fiscal austerity measures can be a better answer to the recessions. However, since 2008 the Irish government used fiscal austerity as a response to the 2008 recession, until the beginning of the year 2012. There was no strong positive sign for Irish economic recovery. Like an increase in the tax liabilities, austerity measures are only a better response to reduce government deficit—but not for stimulating economic growth. The austerity measures cannot stop falling stock prices, which cause firms to delay or cancel planned investments. Stock sales take place because of an increase in the demand, which in turn creates investments, which creates jobs. Austerity measures depress demand, which itself causes a declining level of businesses.

3. Ireland's Economic Recovery since 2008

Instead of stimulating its economy, the Irish government targeted its budget deficit in order to stabilise public finance. In this way, Ireland established an austerity budget, a so-called fiscal consolidation—that is, an economic strategy accompanying cuts in spending and increases in taxes. Since the beginning of the 2008 recession, the Irish government reduced its spending in goods and services, including spending in public servants, roads, national defence, wages, pensions, and social programmes. Moreover, carbon taxes and a tax to petrol and diesel increased. Irish taxpayers continue to pay a high price through massive cuts in public spending and tax increases to household income. In this context, for example, the Irish budget of 2011 reduced expenditures on welfare payments such as on child benefits and on unemployment benefits, and expenditures on public workers were reduced. Additionally, the government reduced health expenditures, and a levy of €200,000 increased on Irish citizens whose income exceeded €1 million. The government also reduced expenditures in road maintenance. In this way, the Department of Enterprise, Trade, and Employment reduced spending by €50 million, and it reduced expenditures to training and the public sector under the aegis of its department. The Department of Environment reduced its expenditures in local government spending, such as expenditures in the social housing investment programme. The Department of Education reduced its spending in funding for the Strategic Innovation Fund and in the rates of student support grants and vocational training opportunity schemes, as well as in other allowances. The reduction in expenditures in the Irish departments, and an increase in taxpayers' income, express Irish government saving.

In this context, the reason of saving is to increase investment. Nevertheless, saving and investment differ from one another. This means that saving does not always involve investment. It is true that when a country saves, it increases its wealth and employment. In this respect, however, a country's saving increases its wealth and employment because the rates of its savings equal the rates to its investment. In other words, when a country increases its wealth and employment, their saving corresponds to its new investment. When a country's saving does not correspond to its new investment, the result is a decrease in country wealth and employment. From this context, the current Irish government savings does not correspond to its new investment—it corresponds to Ireland's debts. Since 2009, Ireland has saved for repayment of its debts, not for new investment. This explains why the Irish economy will take a long time to recover. Even though austerity plays an important role in reducing budget deficit, the Irish economic recovery will not depend on current Irish austerity. Irish economic recovery will occur when the government has paid off its debt and reduced the budget deficit; then it can begin saving for new investments. This would happen when the priority for the government is to increase purchasing power of households and to invest in public services.

4. The Road to Sustainable Job Creation

1. **The government's new plan.** Because recession is strengthened by high unemployment, instead of increasing the age for pensions, the government should consider creating new jobs for young graduates and youth unemployment. New employees increase the consumption of goods and services. For example, new jobs increase spending because employees purchase houses and other necessary, durable goods like auto. Old employees are already equipped, and so they spend less than new employees. In this regard, the age for pensions could be less than sixty-five in both the public and private services. The government can consider increasing the age for pensions if there is no increase in graduates and unemployed youth.

    New jobs would be subsidised by government expenditures cut from unproductive economic sectors, like social welfare services and defence. Moreover, more training for graduates and youths could be a strategy for economic recovery. At this point, training should be based on expectations of trainees, not on expectations of training institutions. Additionally, instead of increasing taxation in household income, governments should consider increasing taxation in luxury goods. As a suggestion, if a household has two houses, the tax of the second house should be considered in taxes increase, but this could be considered as an increase in tax temporarily. Further, a temporary cut of expenses from government and parliament would be necessary for the creation of new jobs. In the government's new plan, the creation of a Permanent Fund for New Job Creation is needed to sustain employment. The role of Permanent Fund for New Job Creation would be to sustain employment during booms and recessions.

2. **Flexibility in tax liabilities on profits.** Flexibility in the tax liabilities in businesses is a crucial strategy to sustain economic

growth and to lessen the effect of recession. Because businesses invest a part of their profits, increases in the investment depend on the profits of businesses. In this context, the reduction in the tax liabilities would increase investment, which itself would increase employment in recession, increase the tax liabilities of businesses during boom period, and create new jobs while lessening the effect of unexpected recession. In other words, a reduction in tax liabilities would increase profits in recession, whereas increases in tax liabilities in the boom period would reduce the likelihood of boom bust. Thus in a boom period, when there is an increase in profits in the business, tax liabilities would be set on high level; in a recession it would be set on low level.

In boom periods, a tax increase in the profits would increase government investment in areas such as education and markets research of new products, which in turn would create new jobs.

3. **Increase innovation.** Recession could happen because of the changing behaviour of consumers in consumption. Accordingly, increasing finances in research will increase a new variety of goods. More varieties of goods in the markets will cause a price reduction, and the reduction will cause a rise in consumption, which itself increases new investments. Although innovations increase capital gain, it also raises the willingness of consumers to spend, and the result is higher sales of goods and services. Furthermore, because innovation reduces the cost to produce goods and services, it would increase the country's exports and tourists within the country. Natural recessions are a result of a lack of innovations, so an increase in innovation will be a strategy which can prevent severe economic downturn.

4. **Increase investment in education.** The result of inequality in education and training is a disparity in income. There are no other solutions for the eradication of disparities in incomes, so investments in education and training could lessen a high disparity in income. In this respect, restructuring funds in social welfare is needed because the consequence of increasing the fund in social welfare is an inequality in income. Funds in social welfare are

unproductive. Despite that, recipients of social welfare contribute to economy by spending their income; they are always dependent on the state. Instead of new investments, the government spends more money in social welfare recipients. New investments are more savings, whereas more spending means an increase in government deficit. At this point, increasing investment in education would encourage young unemployment to be engaged in education and creativity rather than signing on the dole. In this regard, a number of OECD countries have enacted important labour market reforms that have included measures to address the problem of excessive benefit dependency, as well as measures to reinforce labour demand—for example, the relaxation of regulatory rules affecting job protection.[5]

5. **Invest in public construction**. The government should consider investment in roads and other public constructions. For example, Ireland's government should invest in social house building, which would reduce the cost of rent in the private-property houses. In addition to reducing the cost of government rent in private-property houses for social welfare recipients, the government can create jobs in construction while increasing competitiveness in private-property rent.

6. **Economic plan**. In Ireland, the main cause of the 2008 recession was a lack of regulation policy in the housing planning. The government increased investment in the houses without considering the length of its markets; thus the government overestimated the Irish housing markets, which itself caused misallocation of capital. The government allowed developers to build more houses without considering potential buyers of houses. Consequently there was a decline in housing sales. In other words, the lack of buyers of houses caused a decline in the housing sales, so in this context, the government not only overestimated the Irish housing markets, but it also overestimated investment in the housing markets. Therefore, in addition to Irish household indebtedness, unsold houses and

---

[5] See OECD (2009), "The Jobs Crisis: What Are the Implications for Employment and Social Policy?"

unfinished houses revealed incompetence in the Irish housing planning.

7. **Public administration services.** Because public administration influences job creation through their services, it is necessary for governments to implement policies that result performance in public services. Public administration increases economic efficiency when it increases performance in their services.

In general, it is impossible to prevent natural recession in the markets. However, the first indication of incoming recession is an increase in unemployment and high prices in the single segment of market expected to slowdown, so a continuation of the creation of new jobs would lessen the effect of unexpected recession in the markets. Thus a new plan cycle could be the only solution to lessen the effect of natural recession. Better economic management is needed to prevent unnatural recession, and to maintain a country's performance in relation to economic growth, it needs an institution that can monitor economic growth and incoming recession.

There are two types of recession, natural recession and unnatural recession. Natural recession is normal in the markets and is caused by commodities declines in sales, which in turn cause investment to decline. For example, the 2001 recession in America was a natural recession: it was caused by the collapse of the dot-com bubble. The collapse was caused by a decline in investment in the Internet. In other words, the 2001 recession was caused by a decline in sales of computers and software. In this context, a decline in commodities sales can be explained by three elements. The first element is a decline in employment, which itself decreases consumers spending. The second element of decline could be explained by consumer changes in consumption behaviour; instead of purchasing computers and software, consumers direct their spending towards other products. The third element of decline in sales could be explained by disparities in incomes, which cause an imbalance in sales (which itself causes an unstable investment).

High disparities in income could slow down investments, which in turn cause businesses and economic growth to slow down. For example, assume that a country with a population of four million has only one million with a high income, and they are the only people who have purchasing power both in the markets of durable products and in the markets increased in the prices. Thus assume three million with low income have no purchasing power. In this context, assume that the one million with high income spend their income in the markets of computers and software. At this stage, if the population with high income changes its behaviour and instead spends income in the market of automobiles, sales in the markets of computers and software would decline. Moreover, the decline in sales of computers and software would decrease the investment in Internet and employment in Internet; furthermore, employees in the markets of computers and software would lose their jobs. In this way, however, employment in the markets of computers and software would decline, whereas employment in the markets of automobiles would increase. Thus the consequence of disparities in income is an imbalance in employment, which itself causes persistence in unemployment, and persistence in unemployment causes economic growth and businesses to slow down. The result of disparities in income is an unstable investment and an unstable economic growth.

Although natural recession is a consequence of decline in the commodities sales, unnatural recession is a consequence of inefficiencies in policy which causes an increasingly raising market prices. For example, the 2008 recession is an unnatural recession because it originated from inefficient policies that channelled excessive funds in the housing sector markets. The consequences of these excessive funds in the housing markets were an increasingly excessive easing loan in the housing markets, so these excessive easing loans caused rising prices in the housing markets. In turn, an increase in houses prices caused a majority of investors to increase investment in the housing markets. The result of increasing investment in the housing market was an increase in employment in the housing markets and in the financial institutions (banking, insurance companies, etc.). However, the excessive funds in the housing markets depressed other investments because in addition to the creditor increased bonds in the housing markets, more consumer income was directed to repayment of house mortgages and other household requirements.

For example, although the Irish economy was sustained by the single market sector of housing market, this means that Irish job creation was mainly linked to the housing market. Therefore a decline in house sales caused the Irish economy to slow down, which in turn caused unemployment to rise. In this context, an increase in unemployment further decreased retail sales. The decline in the retails sales caused a decline in industry production and investment.

As discussed earlier in this book, employment depends on the profits of markets. In a recession it is hard to sustain employment because markets are in a condition of non-profit, and investors are unwilling to invest. In this situation, there is a need of strategies that can raise investors' profits, which would raise employment. That is, strategies can attract consumers to increase their spending, which raises investors' profits, which in turn causes an increase in investment. However, because characteristics of recessions differ, this explains that strategies for employment in recessions would not be status quo; past solutions to economic recovery cannot be taken as solutions to recover every economy that is in a downturn. Therefore because the origin and effect of recession in markets differ, strategies to be used for economic recovery will differ.

When recession is caused by high rates in the inflation, it takes so long to recover because the central bank raises interest rates to decrease inflation rates. Rising interest rates therefore depress investments because they reduce money in the hands of investors and consumers. Thus high interest rates make investors unwilling to borrow for their investments. Recession caused by inflation is timely on the recovery of the markets themselves, not on government or banking policy; in other words, in addition to the central bank policy of rising interest rates, the economy will recover itself. Unnatural recession takes longer for recovery because it is rooted in the financial problems of consumers. With the exception of market failures, it often happens that a real change of markets begins to occur at around the five-year period.

Table 2

Natural Recession	Unnatural Recession
Cause	**Cause**
Lack of innovation Decline in sales Decline in investment Change of consumers behaviour in spending	Excessive government expenditures Misallocation of capital Inefficiency policy in planning High rates in inflation (high prices) Lack of job creation
Business Recovery	**Business Recovery**
Fast recovery because businesses care for themselves. Markets don't need government intervention.	Recovery takes longer because of financial problems; less liquidity in the market.

4.1. Can Policymakers Prevent Recession?

Although many people argue that recession can be prevented, policymakers cannot prevent natural recession because it is inherently in the market. They can prevent unnatural recession because it originated from inefficient policies of policymakers; because inflation and unemployment are considered as measures of economic progress, policymakers can use it to prevent unnatural recession. In this context, however, policymakers should first decide the limit of the natural rate of unemployment is—that is, the percentage of people who often are out of work and are defined as low unemployment. In this regard, the natural rate of unemployment can be defined as the people who are often the recipients of social welfare.

Suppose that the natural rate of unemployment in Ireland appears to be 4 per cent. From this way, inflation can be considered at a low rate when the unemployment rate is above the natural rate of unemployment. In other words, when the inflation rate is low, it explains high unemployment, and the inflation rate is high when the unemployment rate is less than natural rate of unemployment—say, less than 4 per cent. This explains that the reduction of a natural rate of unemployment raises inflation.

But when inflation is high, it does not always mean that unemployment is less than the natural rate of unemployment. For example, in the 1970s, in the United Kingdom there was high unemployment while the inflation rate was at high level. Inflation rose from 7.1 per cent in 1972 to 24.2 per cent in 1975, and unemployment rose from 4 per cent to over 5 per cent.[6] This example explains that an increase in the inflation rate does not necessarily express low unemployment. At this stage, because high inflation does not always express low employment, it could be useful if policymakers use the level of investment and employment for measuring economic progress. In this perspective, although the level of investment causes unemployment to increase or decrease, policymakers would know whether the economy is growing or slowing down, so they can prevent or lessen the effect of incoming unnatural recession by monitoring investment and employment. Employment increases while the level of investment increases, and vice versa. An increase in investment causes prices to raise, and thus the inflation rate rises, which then causes wages to rise. When wages are not rising, this means that investments are decreasing. For example, when investment in the housing market increase, it causes an increase in employment while increasing prices of houses and wages. In this context, when investments decrease, it explains a decline in job creation, which causes high employment and recession.

In addition, when government revenues are in a decline, it is an indication of a decrease in the country's investment. The big mistakes of policymakers are to wait until unemployment becomes untenable before they intervene. To stop an increase in unemployment, policymakers need to define the limit of the natural rate of unemployment. Therefore, based on the natural rate of employment, policymakers can know if investments are progressing or declining.

One can ask how ordinary people can recognise that their country is sinking in recession. In addition to many people losing their jobs

---

[6]   Source: United Kingdom Office for National Statistics. See Mankiw, N. G. and Taylor, M. P. (2007), *Macroeconomics: European Edition*, New York: Worth Publishers, p. 402.

and an absence of hiring new people, particularly young graduates, tax increases in the public services and the introduction of new public service charges are crucial indications that the country is sinking in recession.

4.2. Can Governments Raise Confidence in the Markets?

Since the 2008 international recession, European governments have been working hard in order to raise confidence in the markets—that is, making markets to operate in the normal way, selling and buying without decline. However, until now they are still implementing strategies that can make markets operate as normal. To discuss what strategy can cause markets to operate in the normal way, it is necessary to start with understanding how markets work.

In general, markets are composed of four stages. The first stage is based on the owners of capital: the bankers, governments, insurance companies, and other privates sectors. The second stage is the producers who produce markets, goods, and services. The third stage is the suppliers and retailers. The finally stage is the consumers. Although the owners of the capitals are the principal lenders in the markets, producers borrow capital from them. In the markets, producers can supply their goods to the suppliers on credit. The suppliers also can deliver their merchandises on credits to the retailers. Therefore when the relationship between producers and suppliers, and the relationship between suppliers and retailers, is positive, markets are operating in the normal function and thus are selling and buying. In this way, the markets are in the right way of profits, and the lenders are ready to mortgage the markets. Moreover, because of the increase in retailers' sales, it expresses the increase in the quantity of production. However, planned quantity of production depends on profits. When the profit in the production is less than the profit expected, the producers reduce production.

For example, suppose that Dell produces new desktop computers. An increase in sales of Dell computers in the markets means that Dell might increase its production. But an increase in the production depends on the profits from the computers Dell produces. If profits are less than expected on computers produced, Dell has to reduce production. As a consequence, the markets of selling and buying Dell computers will decline; this will follow by a decline in the prices of Dell computers. In this situation, Dell would restructure its planned production, to make redundant use of its employees in the production of the computers. Subsequently, there might be a decline in employment in the markets of Dell computers. In this context, the recession starts from decline in the sales, which in turn causes employees to lose their jobs. In this condition, the policymakers' governments can intervene in order to restore or raise the Dell market. Thus, because the profits of Dell computers depends on the cost of computers produced, the policymakers can intervene by decreasing the cost of producing computers. In this respect, because in businesses, expenses such as workers wages have to be taken from profits, governments respond by cutting workers' wages. To maintain employment in the markets of Dell computers, it is necessary to cut Dell workers' wages, which in turn causes Dell to regain profits in its production, which further causes Dell computers to increase in the market. Moreover, governments can intervene by reducing Dell's tax in each computer produced.

Without government intervention, however, there is the likelihood that prices in the market adjust itself, and the increase in production of Dell computers would resume when Dell saw the opportunity to regain profits in its computers produced. But this opportunity can happen if there is an increase in job creation in other areas of markets, to compensate for jobs loss in the Dell market. For example, as noted earlier, the 2001 recession was caused by a decline in the investment in internet between 1995 and 2001, which itself caused a decline in the sales of computer and software. The 2001 recession recovered because of growing investment in the housing markets from 1990s to 2007.

Finally, a decline in sales can cause producers to introduce new products in the market, which in itself can drive consumers to increase consumption. In the Dell production context, a decrease in the sales of Dell computers could cause Dell to reshape their computers in order to increase its sales, or make a new product line (such laptop computers) to offset the profits decline in the sales of its previous computers.

In other words, without government intervention, producers can increase demand in the market. For example, assume that producers who produce black jeans to the consumers in the age fifty group have learned that sales of black jeans declined while the sales of khaki jeans rose. At this stage, instead of producing black jeans, producers will produce the khaki jeans. In this context, because the recession starts from a decline in sales, governments can raise confidence in the markets by increasing the purchasing power of consumers, thus increasing consumer demand in the markets. The government can increase the purchasing power of consumers by reducing tax charges on their income. This explains that the confidence of markets is based on the increasing demand of consumers, not on government spending or austerity. Government can increase consumers' demand in the markets by sustaining job creation. One can ask why the Eurozone governments were unable to sustain job creation during the 2008 recession. This was because of the increase in budget deficit in Eurozone governments; some Eurozone governments were unable to support job creation while maintaining current expenditures.

In general, government can raise confidence in the markets by raising the confidence of consumers, by raising their purchasing power. Although government spending is necessary and efficient in welfare sectors, government spending raises confidence in individuals' businesses when it is directed in productive sectors that create jobs.

Chapter References

Labonte and Makinen (2002), "The Current Economic Recession: How Long, How Deep, and How Different from the Past?" CRS Report for Congress, Code RL31237.

Labonte and Makinen (2008), "Monetary Policy and the Federal Reserve: Current Policy and Conditions", Code RL30354.

Kliesen K. L. (2003), "The 2001 Recession: How Was It Different and What Developments May Have Caused It?" Federal Reserve, Bank of St Louis.

Velde F. R. (2009), "The Recession of 1937—A Cautionary Tale", *Economic Perspectives*, Federal Reserve Bank of Chicago.

CHAPTER II

Business

Working Three Years as a Wholesaler

Wholesalers are defined as businesses that buy goods from producers and manufacturers and from other firms at low prices, then resell the goods to retailers at higher prices. When I was working in the wholesale shop, we sold our goods to regular customers with different behaviour. We developed our own sales strategy so that within one hour after opening our wholesale, we used to find information about selling prices in other wholesales with similar merchandise. And because it was the customers who were driving our prices, we used to see whether prices changed by observing if there was an unusual drop or rise in buying our goods. If there was a dramatic increase in buying our goods, this was the signal that the prices of our goods were increased at other wholesale shops, and vice versa. In this context, we used to increase prices because other wholesale increased their prices. Moreover, we increased prices because there was an increase in buying our goods, or because our suppliers warned us about a shortage of goods. In the period we sold more goods, it was necessary to hire more workers as temporary workers. Furthermore, we used to introduce new items in our store if we found that the items were more profitable.

Dell's European Manufacturing Computers

Dell's European manufacturing was set up in Limerick, Ireland, in 1990, but the official opening took place in 1991. The Dell computers were destined for direct delivery to retailers and public service offices, and also to private services offices in Europe, the Middle East, and Africa.

In 2008 I was offered a job in Dell's European manufacturing facility in Limerick. As a worker with flexible working hours; I used to work in the normal and exceptional hours. I used to work for eight hours, but some days I worked twelve hours, and sometimes it was less than eight hours. Working twelve hours was a signal that Dell had an increase in demand, and thus people and offices were buying more Dell computers. Working less than eight hours was a signal that demand was on the decrease—people and offices were buying less Dell computers. Within four months, Dell computer sales were up and down. In this respect, Dell was hiring and laying off workers according to Dell computer demand. When there was an increasing in demand, Dell used to renew the contracts of its workers and hired new workers, and vice versa. I was among the workers who signed a new contract at the end of August 2008, but for personal reasons I decided to ask for the termination of my contract in early October 2008. At this time there was no indication that Dell would close down. However, because of the 2008 international financial crisis and the recession in Ireland, Dell closed down its computers manufacturing in Limerick in 2009.

In addition to the high cost of Dell labour in Ireland in the beginning of the 2008 crisis, Dell closed down because its computer sales were in decline. In other words, Dell closed down its plant in Ireland because, since the 2008 economic crisis, its business was no longer profitable in Ireland.

1. How Businesses Create Jobs

Without exception, a country's economic growth is driven by high rates of employment, and the rates of employment depend on its goods and service as well as its productivity. An increase in the country's productivity depends on the specialisation of goods and services that a country produces. Thus if the country produces goods and services consumed more in domestic or international markets, this means that the country will increase trade which itself, and employment will rise. When goods and services have a low production cost, they are increased in demand both domestically and internationally. Moreover, a high productivity is created by smart services and smart bureaucracy in the financial services and communications services, as well as transportation services.

The second way of how businesses create jobs is the relative total cost of producing goods and services. The relative comparative costs in production determine the creation of jobs in a country. For example, if goods and services produced in Ireland cost more than goods and services produced in Luxembourg, this means that Luxembourg will create more jobs and Ireland will create fewer jobs. Luxembourg will increase employment because its goods and services cost less in the markets. Thus, the low price of goods and services produced in Luxembourg will cause Luxembourg trade to rise at a high level, which in turn causes high employment. In contrast, because services and goods in Ireland are relative costly to be produced, Ireland's services and goods will be relatively traded at a high price, and this might cause Ireland to lose the markets, which in turn causes the slowdown of employment. In this context, Ireland's strategy to increase employment would be to cut the cost of producing its goods and services. It is certain that in this situation, a wage cut is the third way of job creation because of discount in both the cost of production of goods and the cost of services; as a result, wages cut is an increase in the profits of businesses. Goods and services produced at low prices cause an increase in trade, which itself raises the profits in businesses. A high level in trade in turn causes businesses to increase employment.

Assume that a personal computer made in Ireland in the market would be sold at €450, whereas a personal computer made in Luxembourg would be sold at €400. In this case, a personal computer from Luxembourg would be sold at a lower price because it costs less to make it; in Ireland a personal computer would be sold at a higher price because it costs more to make it. A Dell facility in Luxembourg would increase employment because its trade and sale of personal computers would rise at a high level. By contrast, in Ireland Dell would cut employment because its sales would be at a low level.

Moreover, wage cuts increase investments because all expenses in the businesses are deducted from businesses profits, and cut wages increases business profits. At this stage, businesses would create more jobs but increase profits. This explains why an increase in the profits of a country's stock market raises a country's employment, and vice versa.

Suppose that Dell's profits in the sale and trade of personal computers was €100,000 per week, and workers' wages was €50,000 per week. Instead of €100,000 profit per week, Dell's net profit per week would be €50,000. Then, assume that Dell cut the wages of its workers to €30,000. At this stage, its net profits would be €70,000.

In this respect, Dell's profits rise to €70,000 per week from €50,000. In this condition there is a probability that Dell would reinvest more profit in its business, which in turn would cause Dell to increase employment. In this way, as long as businesses increase profits in stock, the increase in profits would increase investments, which would cause high employment and economic growth. In turn, economic growth in the long term would cause rising prices in the markets, which causes an increase in wages. In this context, cutting wages is necessary when there is a price decline in the market, because declines in market prices cause a decrease in business profits. It is always necessary to introduce wage cuts when business profits fall. Thus in addition to the rise in unemployment during the slowdown of economic growth, it is required to cut wages that were increased in the period of growth. An increase in business profits means an increase in wages, so a decrease in profits does not mean only a decrease in job creation, but it also means a decrease in wages.

Unemployment is a result of a decrease in business profits, which itself causes the slowdown of businesses. Furthermore, declines in businesses cause the gross domestic product to decline, which in turn causes a deficit in country revenue.

Another strategy of job creation is low interest rates, which cause investors to increase their investment and consumers to increase their consumptions. An increase in investments and consumptions causes a rise in employment. In this regard, low taxes such as corporation tax can facilitate job creation. The low taxes not only encourage country entrepreneurs to create businesses, but it stimulates foreign direct investments. Tax cuts are crucial for employment.

Assume that Dell's profits before taxes is €200,000. If Dell's tax liabilities per year equals €40,000, this means Dell's net profits per year is €160,000. Suppose that the government decides to cut Dell's tax liabilities from €40,000 per year to €20,000. Dell's net profits would be €180,000 per year. At this stage, there is an increase of €20,000 in Dell's net profits per year: instead of €160,000, Dell would invest €180,000. In this respect, the increases in employment depends on the net profit increase in Dell. Increasing Dell's net profits means an increase in Dell's job creation. In this condition, as Dell gains more profits, the country gain an increase in employment.

Another example is for the government to cut income tax. At this point income tax cuts increase the purchasing power of consumers, which in turn increases consumption, and increases in consumption causes an increase in investment. Suppose that the government's tax liabilities on a household earning €2,040 per week equals €20. A household's net income tax per week would be €2,020 per week. Again assume that the household expenses per week equals €1500, and this household would save €520 per week. Because €520 is both saving and investment, both the household's spending and savings would increase employment. However, suppose the government decides to cut taxes liabilities from €20 to €10. This means that the net income of households would increase to €2,030 At this point, instead of €520, the household would save €530.

Finally, another strategy of job creation is government investment in infrastructures such as roads, broadband, housing, offices, and the reconstruction of government institutions. Like private equity, government spending causes an increase in employment. A country's infrastructure not only encourages foreign direct investments, but it reduces the cost of goods and services and also increases capability of domestic businesses. Moreover, the government should consider creating an environment that makes investors want to lend their money to producers and traders.

2. Increase Employment in the Small- and Medium-Sized Enterprises

According to economist Lori Kletzner, within an industry a 10 per cent increase in sales due to exports leads to a 7 per cent increase in employment, whereas a 10 per cent increase in domestic demand leads to just a 3-5 per cent increase in employment.[7] This fact explains why small- and medium-sized enterprises (SMEs) can create more jobs when they are able to export their goods. In this respect, it is possible that SMEs could be unable to export their goods because of a lack of enough capital to finance the transaction of export services, when their foreign clients need them to pay transaction services on their goods. At this stage, credit financing of SMEs' transaction in export services of goods could be key to energising enterprises to increase exports. Thus, a bank dedicated to financing small- and medium-sized enterprises is necessary to support them in their exports while creating jobs. This could happen if policymakers can view SMEs as effective businesses to create jobs, because access to credit is often quoted as one of the main challenges facing SMEs.

---

[7]   See United States House of Representatives Committee on Financial Service Subcommittee on International Monetary Policy and Trade, "Testimony of Mathew Slaughter-legislative proposals on securing American jobs through export: Export-Import Bank Reauthorisation", 24 May, 2011.

Moreover, because default is a major source of risk in many small businesses, it is necessary to set up an institution appropriate to support small-business entrepreneurs. This management institution can work as an institution supporting entrepreneurs' services. In order to facilitate the development and strengthening of the small-business sector, training support services and institutions to represent the interests of entrepreneurs is necessary. Additionally, because one of the main barriers of small businesses is a lack of information and the capacity to adapt to changing market conditions, the support from institutions should not be dispersed over many institutions, because small businesses have to contact multiple institutions in order to solve a particular problem. In other words, services dedicated to supporting small businesses can increase performance in small businesses if they are provided by private providers rather than the government. In this context, entrepreneurs should be able to easily find appropriate providers of small- and medium-sized supports; this would enhance SMEs to identify service expertise in their businesses. Furthermore, implementation of sound accounting systems and regular reporting are necessary for bank loans to businesses. The role of government in SMEs is to ensure that more transparency and accountability are considered above political interests in boards dedicated to support services in SMEs.

CHAPTER III

▼

Political Party Ways to Facilitate
Job Creation

During political party campaigns for general election, mainly in a period of economic downturn, Social Democrats, Labour Parties, and Socialist Parties argue that the creation of jobs requires government spending and an increase in taxation. Conservatives Parties and the right-wing parties argue that the creation of jobs requires savings and low taxation, as well as wage cuts. Further, because of a country's budget deficit, policymakers argue that the state could create jobs on the basis of consolidation, thus increasing taxation while cutting spending. Political party arguments are explained on the basis of different ideologies, so to better understand their arguments, it is necessary to explore the ideology of different political party to be able to understand their arguments about job creation. Understanding the ideology of political parties is necessary because it helps understand what a political party expects to accomplish after being elected, and during the campaign voters can argue and challenge politicians in a real debate about the standard of living. Moreover, because bad choices of voters in electing representatives downgrades the country's economic growth, understanding political party ideology might help voters to choose politicians who can contribute more to their society than weaken their standard of living and their society. At this stage, I argue that voting could be better if voters voted on the basis of individuals' accountability rather than on the basis of political party or majority opinions, or common-sense morality. The next sections discuss the ideologies of political parties and what they expect to accomplish after being elected.

1.   Conservatives versus Social Democrats

Political parties express their arguments on the basis of either socialism ideology or conservatism ideology. Political parties that argue on the basis of socialism ideology include the Labour Party, the Social Democratic Party, and the Socialist Party. In the political arena, these political parties are called the left wing political parties, and its sympathizers are named socialists. In the United States of America, socialist parties are viewed as communists.

Political parties that argue on the basis of conservative ideology include the American Republican Party and Britain's Conservative Party, or Tories. In this political arena, these political parties are called the right wing political parties, and its sympathizers are called conservatives.

The terms left and right originated from the French Revolution and were termed according to the seating arrangement of the different groups at the first meeting of the Estates-General in 1789. Nobles who supported the king sat to his right, whereas members of the Third Estate sat to his left. Today, socialists are viewed as revolutionary or egalitarian; conservatives are viewed as militants who do not like change. In terms of economic strategy, the left parties are viewed as committed to equality, whereas the right parties are viewed as committed to individuals and their businesses. In other words, socialists believe in government intervention in employment, and conservatives want to negate government intervention in employment. For a better understanding of the left and right parties' policies in the political arena, let us start with a short summary of the origin of the French Revolution and the economic development of 1800s England.

1.2. Origin of the French Revolution

During the eighteenth century, France was largely a feudal society: Its society was characterised by countryside, agriculture, and landholding, and also the absence of town and French cities. France's economies were mainly based on a system of land holding structured on agricultural economy, and on a system of social relations established on class distinctions between the landholder and the serf cultivator. The economic activity in feudal society was the production of food supply structured on the basis of a system of land holding based on social relations and subordination between the landholder and the serf. In this respect, there were five distinct social economic systems.

1. The system gave power to landholders to transform the serf into slavery.
2. The legal subordination of serfs to the lord.
3. The right of the landholder to obtain control over agricultural production of the serf.
4. The right of the landholder to impose taxes on the serf.
5. The social hierarchy and class distinctions supported by legal and religious sanctions. At this point, serfs were in an obligation system, controlled by the lord's household. There were specific tasks imposed on the serfs during certain days of the year.

Overall in the eighteenth century, the French economy was booming and prices were rising and although, in 1787, French economy was in slowdown, in that year there was an indication of economic recovery. Nevertheless, because of poor crops, there were shortages of foods which caused prices of food to rise. Despite wage increase, real wages went in decline relative to an increase in the prices of food and other goods. Additionally, government revenue was in deficits. Furthermore, because of poor harvests between the year of 1788 and 1789, prices rose further. Because of increasingly state deficits, at this stage, the financiers were reluctant to lend. As result, this raised unemployment at high level. Moreover, there was a shortage of bread in the cities and in the countryside. Therefore, despite government intervention which decreased prices of bread in Paris, French people; entrepreneurs, businessmen, manufacturers and farmers were impatient. An increase of shortage of food and unemployment caused the beginning of the revolution.

In the beginning of 1789, citizens formed a Revolutionary Committee and submitted a set of demands for change to the central authority of the French Estates-General, which was composed of nobles, clergy, and the peasants. In response, the king called a meeting of Estates-General, and the resolution of this meeting was a voting procedure. However, by June 1789 the Third Estate split off from the Estates-General, proclaiming a new political body named the National Assembly. From June to July of 1789, despite military intervention, riots swept France. As a result, the French Revolution ended a feudal society. The National Assembly drafted the Declaration of the Rights of Man, which stated that all human beings were born free and equal in their political rights, regardless of their class position. Furthermore, the declaration terminated the subordination system between French people; thus all social systems based on feudal social distinctions was terminated. As the political change started to take effect, there was an eradication of French feudal society, and all legal forms were brought to a democratic republic based on the rights of citizens. In other words, the capitalistic institutions replaced the feudal institutions.

1.3. Economic Development of 1800s England

Similar to France, the way of life in England was based on a legal form of feudal society. There also was an absence of large towns. The production of food supply dominated everyday life: while serf cultivators laboured on their own holdings for their economic needs, they also performed unpaid service to benefit the lord's estate. There was no private property; instead, there was a system of customary linking individuals to each other and to the land. But in this system, distinctions in use of land existed. There were estate lands which included the lord's agricultural holdings. Moreover, there was a land called open field, which the serfs used. There was a land denoted common fields, which were commonly used for grazing domestic animals. However, in the beginning of the middle of the sixteenth century, economic changes started to have an effect on these systems of feudal economy. At the first stage of change, there was the enclosure movement and a transfer of the population from countryside economy to the town economy, which is industry economy. In this regard, land enclosures meant that landholders transformed a system of customary to private property. Therefore the enclosure of land can be termed as a system whereby tenant holdings in feudal land and agriculture became enclosed and were made available for the private use of the landholder. Peasant families were evicted from their holdings. The enclosure was followed by a system of tenant holdings by landholders. The second stage was to transform the countryside economy, and thus the feudal economy, to a town economy. The third stage was the decline of the power of the trade guilds. The final stage was completed with the transformation of countryside economy to town economy, and thus modern economy. Although the countryside was based on agricultural economy and common knowledge, the town economy was based on enterprises and self-knowledge.

In the beginning of 1710, Parliament enacted the first Enclosure Bill to legalise enclosure of tenant holdings. Subsequently, in the early 1800s, Parliament enacted four thousand acts. Consequently the rates of enclosures accelerated, and displaced populations transferred to the cities. Moreover, enclosures caused a movement which separated peasants from their standard of life: living based on their own agricultural holdings. At this stage, only landholders were entitled to rights of modern private property. In this context, the land was transformed into commercial commodity. Although money rents replaced labour rents, peasants were forced to make money for their standard of living. This was the starting point to end the feudal system. Peasant populations were transferred in a system of industrial production, which was based on wages labour. Therefore as the industrial production began to increase, there was a market economy for buying and selling commodities. At this stage, class interests started to emerge and caused the need for state administration. But as the peasant population moved from countryside to towns to work in industries, there was increased unemployed in the towns, which led to the formation of social policy directed to the problems of the industrial workers, such as their living conditions and the problems of over-population. Further, social institutions related to family were established. Due to economic changes, a way of living was also changed. Economic development was accompanied with the process of individualism. After land enclosures, each peasant was self-directed to move from countryside to town to look for jobs. Moreover, every peasant was in a self-seeking new way of life. So in principal, individualism refers to the process of self-determination—and to the way of self-help. At this point, while capitalism institutions were established to regulate conditions of living in towns, it was the family or individual's interests to look for a job and choose his own way of living.

The term "individualism" was first used by Joseph de Maistre and Henri Saint-Simon to criticise the dominance of the individual over social and political institutions, which occurred after the French Revolution. Today, the dominance of individuals over capitalistic institutions is still blooming and is the main cause of recessions in the world markets. Thus, in addition to the cause of inequality in capitalism society, this problem is the origin of civil war in developing countries and riots in developed countries. Today governments are influenced by a few corporate individuals.

Though many would agree that capitalism is based on an economic system that functions differently from the feudal economic system, some define capitalism as itself a free market. Capitalism is a social system that recognizes individuals' rights of ownership and that is based on democratic institutions; thus capitalism institutions are characterised by ownership of the means of production, labour, and free markets. In feudal society, there was no recognition of individuals' ownership. Moreover, citizens were under the command of their governor. However, in capitalism citizens have the right to exchange information with their governor. In feudal societies, citizens were associated with common economic activity and collective markets; thus citizens were imposed to do what their governor wanted. By contrast, in capitalism societies citizens are self-directed and have a right to choose their own businesses. In this respect, free markets were associated with an individual's capability, so capitalism associates individuals to private ownership, whereas free markets associate the individual with know-how. Though private ownership is a principle of capitalism, free markets are characterised by competitiveness. In this context, conservatives' policies are about the individual know-how, whereas socialists' policies are about the rights of individuals. In this respect, basic principles of socialists originated from the French Revolution, and basic principles of conservatives are originated from historically economic development in 1800s England. Despite that, conservatives and socialists recognize the necessity of capitalism. Conservatives mislead the principles of capitalism; instead, they view capitalism as modern institutions that regulate individuals' rights, and as institutions with markets without regulation. The meaning of capitalism is not a free market. Capitalism means a society with modern institutions. Free markets allow individuals to choose their own business according to their capability, while respecting capitalism institutions that regulate fraud and corruption in the world's free markets.

2. Conservatives' Ways to Facilitate Job Creation

In general, conservative policy is basically built on business ownership, and they often don't like political change. Conservatives view business ownership as a benefit for capitalism institutions; it is a good way to obey capitalism law and the businesses of others. Thus the conservative preference is individuals' enterprises over state enterprises, and they consider nationalisation policy as an inefficient strategy for economic health. They believe that high profits from individual enterprises will boost economic grow and increase employment; the right way of job creation is to increase capital gains in private equity. Conservatives pledge individuals' self-directed and free markets as the main drive of economic growth; in this respect, they argue that social welfare is bad policy for the country. Social welfare creates a culture of dependence on the country and weakens a country's economic growth. Conservatives not encourage transfer of payments, and thus they do not like to increase funds in the institutions such as social security, unemployment compensation, and social welfare; however, they do not explain clearly about their views on funding education and training. It is true that transfer payments decrease economic growth because they are funds without return. But if conservatives view funds in education and training as the same as the transfer payments in social welfare, this is a weakness in conservative strategy because the foundation of economic growth is basically sustained by education, training, and know-how.

On taxation, instead of high taxation, conservatives prefer low taxation. As discussed earlier, low taxation increases profits of businesses, which in turn boost employment. Conservatives think that raising taxes is against the free market.

During economic downturn, conservatives prefer fiscal austerity—that is, cutting government expenditures and wages. Wages are considered government expenditures, so an increase in wages means a rise in government expenditures. When the government is in deficit, increasing wages increases the government deficit. Where government deficit is a result of a decline in government income, this means that the government will borrow for its expenditures. At this stage the continuation of increase in the government expenditures would increase government deficit and debts.

On budget deficit, conservatives believe that cutting government expenditures will reduce the budget deficit because during an economic downturn, many businesses close down because of a rise in unemployment. Therefore, in addition to a decline in business tax liabilities, employment tax liabilities decline, which in turn causes government revenue to decline.

Example: **Table 1**: Government Deficit (Increase Government Spending)

Government year income, in € million	Government year expenditures in € million	Balance
100	50	50
10	50	10
10	20	(deficit)

Table 2: Deficit Reduction (Cut Government Expenditures)

Government year income in € million	Government year expenditure in € million	Balance
100	20	80
10	20	70
10	20	60 (New investment: Savings)

Table 1 shows that an increase in government expenditures causes deficit. When a government budget is in deficit, a rise in government expenditures increases government debts, and this means that the government will borrow money for its expenditures. Table 2 shows that a decrease in expenditures reduces deficit.

A €60 million savings is new government investment. However, if the government is already in debt, the government will consider the €60 million savings as payment to its creditors. In this way, the government would be unable to create jobs. Moreover, a decrease in government expenditures does not ensure job creation, because a decrease in government expenditures reduces consumer spending, which itself is a cause for businesses to close down. Only consumer spending can create jobs. *Decreases in government expenditures ensure only a reduction in government deficit and government debts.*

To increase consumer spending, conservatives prefer tax cuts. Tax cuts increase government budget deficit because the cuts decrease government income. So in addition to a reduction in the government's expenditures, tax cuts will cause government debts to increase. Although that tax cut strategy can expand consumer spending, which itself increases businesses and employment, the result of the tax cuts in the long run is a budget deficit and debt. In the long run, employment depends on a country's economic stability.

In the same context, countries that base their economic growth on exports need stability in the countries where they export their goods and services. In other words, all country exporters should have interests in stabilising their partners in businesses.

On bank regulation, conservatives prefer bank deregulation, but they express deregulation to somehow mean free markets, so they do not accept regulation in free market. However, among the principles of capitalism, institutions are to eliminate fraud and corruption in the free markets, as well as to regulate social problems. In other words, governments regulate fraud and corruption in the free markets as well as litigation in businesses. Government regulation is needed in free market because it lessens fraud and corruption in the financial sector. Even though government regulation does not eliminate fraud and corruption in the financial sector, it weakens fraud and corruption in free markets.

Moreover, because the liquid of bank assets are the saving of depositors, individuals, or businesses, regulation is about how banks manage the depositors' saving. This is because irregularity in the bank management would not only cause the loss of depositors' savings, but it would cause bankruptcy. So although banks lend, they should hold enough capital for depositors; because they should be able to withdraw their savings at any time. Table 3 shows a bank balance sheet with enough capital.

Table 3: **Bank Balance Sheet of a Bank with Enough Capital**

Assets	Liabilities (Bank Funds)
Reserves €10 million	Deposits €90 million
Investments (Loans) €90 million	Bank Capital €10 million

Table 3 show reserves of €10 million. Every bank should have reserves; thus according to the rules of bank regulation, every bank should deduct a certain fraction from every cash deposit at the bank. This fraction is called bank required reserves, and it increases accordingly with cash deposits at the banks. Reserves are money liquid of banks assets and are used by banks to meet their obligations. As an example, in Table 3, reserves are €10 million, and this reserve is 10 per cent of the €100 million deposits at the bank. Before deduction of this reserve, the cash deposits in this bank were €100 million, and after the deduction of reserves, deposits equal €90 million. This €90 million is bank money for loans, and this means that in a boom, when the economy is in good health, the €90 million would be in circulation as mortgages instead of sitting in the bank. Table 3 also shows a €10 million bank capital: this is the profits of the bank. Although profits equal the difference between total asset and liabilities, profits are equal to reserve requirements, and bank profits increase when deposits increase. At this point, after a thorough investigation of the markets, the bank must choose whether or not to reinvest its profits. This is a point where irregularity in lending causes banks to fail. Irregularities in the bank lending means lending without considering the bank's rules of lending; the irregularity is often based on clientelism. Thus without considering the bank rules of lending, this can often cause excessive lending. In Ireland, the Anglo-Irish Bank failed because of excessive lending to developers—that is, excessive lending to the housing market.

Based on the above context, assume that the bank decides to reinvest €10 million profits in loans. At this stage, if repayments to the bank fail because of a market failure, this means that the bank is in a situation of bankruptcy. Additionally, suppose that €10 million is withdrawn by depositors. Similarly, the bank is in a state of bankruptcy. Remember, €90 million is in circulation and thus is in the hand of businesses. The bank balance sheets in Table 4 show the state of bank failure. In other words, because depositors withdraw their cash from the bank, the bank will fail. In addition, the bank fails because of an irregularity in its lending. Irregularities in lending cause the bankers to lend bank reserve requirements.

Table 4: **Balance Sheet of Bank Failure**

Assets	Liabilities (Bank funds)
Reserves €10 million	Deposits € 90 million
Loans € 90 Million	Bank capital—€ 10 million

Table 4 shows that bank capital was €10 million was and withdrawn by the depositors. The balance sheet shows that the bank has neither reserve requirements nor bank capital—the bank is in a situation of bankruptcy. In this context, because bank failures are caused by personnel who manage the bank, in order to fix the bank failure, policymakers could chose to close the bank or bail out the failure. At this point, it is not clear what solution conservatives would prefer in relation to bank failure. Both conservatives and social democrats often bail out the bank, but in general conservatives prefer bailout over nationalisation. But in relation to businesses, although American conservatives prefer closing down the businesses in failure, European conservatives and social democrats prefer bailing out those businesses.

3. Social Democrats' Ways to Facilitate Job Creation

As mentioned earlier, social democrat policy originated from socialism ideology. Historically, the basis of socialism ideology was a reaction to deplorable conditions of the manufacturing workers and the unemployed who suffered poverty in the beginning of capitalism. The socialists' commitment was influenced by conditions in which the industrial working class lived and worked; in this context, socialism emerged as a critique of the economy based on individualism. In addition, wages were low and the working day was long. The threat to industry workers was aggravated by the absence of institutions that could help the unemployed and the industrial workers to live in fair conditions. From this context, socialists sought a radical change. For instance, Charles Fourier in France and Robert Owen in Britain encouraged the establishment of communities committed to cooperation and love rather than individual competition and greed. Socialists believe that the natural relationship should be based on cooperation instead of competition. In addition, Karl Marx and Friedrich Engels developed theories that criticised capitalism's social class hierarchy. In the late nineteenth century, socialists' commitment improved working-class living conditions and ended up developing capitalist institutions. In this way, the standard of living conditions of trade unions, working class political parties, and social clubs were enhanced, and the working class was better integrated within industrial society. In addition, the twentieth century witnessed the spread of socialist ideology in African, Asia, and Latin American countries. In these countries, socialists were committed to eradicating colonialism oppression.

In Marx's view, the capitalistic social class is linked to economic power, so social class divisions are based on the separation of individuals' economic activity. In other words, social class divisions are based on ownership of business and labour—that is, between bourgeoisie and the workers who live off the sale of their labour, the proletariat. At this point Marxist theories thought that because the two classes were characterised by irreconcilable conflict, this would lead to the overthrow of capitalism through a proletarian revolution. Moreover, Marx thought that state property should be used for the benefit of humanity rather than individualism. In this context, when Lenin and Bolsheviks seized power in Russia in 1917, they believed that socialism ideology could be built through nationalization (i.e., direct state control over economy). In this respect, Stalin's economy was based on planned economy. At this point, common ownership in feudal society became socialist state property in Russia, while it became state ownership in the West. In this way, Western nationalisation was based on the construction of mixed economy, in which some businesses would control by ownership while others would be state owned. Thus today, despite increasing business ownership, the state still has power in some business ownership, and social democrats represent the interests of the labour society and are committed to helping unemployment.

Social democrats stand for a balance between the ownership of enterprises and the state. Moreover, social democracy recognizes capitalist institutions as the only capable way to increase job creation. Thus social democrats prefer capitalism institutions over business ownership. Whereas conservatives view business ownership as a benefit for capitalism institutions, social democrats view capitalist institutions as a benefit for business ownership. Moreover, while the conservatives' commitment is about particular business, the social democrats' commitment is about the weak and vulnerable. Social democrats' particular principles are based on state welfare, whereas conservatives' particular principles are based on businesses. Social democrats believe that human inequality is a result of a society which based its economic activity on social class hierarchy. It is at this stage that social democrats consider intervention of government necessary for job creation. Although conservatives do not explain clearly whether they agree to increase funds in education and training, social democrats are committed to increase funds in education and training. In general, instead of business ownership, social democrats are committed to state-balanced economics, to free markets and planned economics. In other words, whereas social democrats are committed to the intervention of government in individuals' economic activity, conservatives are against government intervention.

On taxation, social democrats prefer to increase taxes on high-income individuals as well as businesses earning significant profits. In regard to the business profits, however, social democrats don't take into consideration that increasing profits leads to the creation of more jobs. Reinvesting profits means an increase in job creation. Similarly, individuals earning high income create more jobs than individuals with low income; this is because individuals with high income spend more while they increase their saving. As discussed previously, both an increase in the spending and an increase in the saving are the only ways for creating jobs. Many could ask how individuals and groups with high income would create jobs. As already shown, banks obtain funds from individuals and businesses; through these funds, banks create more jobs by lending. Thus because individuals with high income are the ones who have high savings in the bank while spending more than individuals with low income, in turn the high-income people create more jobs than those with low income.

During economic downturn, social democrats' commitment is an increase in taxation; they prefer raising taxes on both high-income individuals and businesses earning high profits. The dilemma here is that although they raise the income tax, they decrease both the spending and savings of individuals and businesses. Though social democrats increase government savings by taxing more the businesses and individuals, they decrease job creation. In the short term, a low taxation can cause economic recovery, but a high taxation cannot because a rise in taxes decreases the profits of businesses, and without profits, businesses are unable to engage in new investment. Regarding bank failure, European social democrats would prefer nationalisation of banks over bailout, whereas in North America, both conservatives and democrats prefer bailing out failed financial institutions.

On budget deficit, social democrats believe that an increase in taxation reduces budget deficit. This is a second way of ensuring a reduction in government deficit and government debts. Nevertheless, increased taxes during economic downturn raises unemployment because it decreases individuals' and businesses' spending and saving. Moreover, social democrats contend that a rise in government expenditure during economic downturns increases employment. At this stage, however, an increase in government spending during economic downturn will not lead to economic recovery without investment and consumer spending.

On bank regulation, social democrats are keen on bank regulation; however, they regard bank regulation to be about allowing mortgages for individuals earning relatively high income, and rejecting individuals who earn low income or are unemployed. In contrast, in Ireland the 2008 debts crisis was caused by excessive loans to the housing market and individuals earning a relatively high income.

4. The Liberals' Ways to Facilitate Job Creation

In the United States, "liberal" means big government because the liberal ideologies include an increase in government spending in the social sector. Liberal ideology is drawn on the construction of a society within which individuals can develop according to the best of her or his ability. In other words, liberals advance the idea that individuals should make their own moral decisions. The liberal commitment is to ensure that every individual is able to act accordingly to her or his interests. In this context, because individuals do not possess the same levels of talent or the same willingness to work, liberals support the principle of meritocracy, which reflects talent and hard work. Liberals believe that the free market allows individuals to develop accordingly to their merit; they advocate industrialised and market economy free from government interference, in which businesses would be allowed to pursue profits. Many liberals view society as a collection of individuals and everyone seeking to satisfy her or his own needs and interests. They believe that individuals possess a social responsibility for one another, especially for those who are unable to look after themselves. All liberals are committed to creating a society in which an individual is capable of supporting himself/herself.

In the above context, Adam Smith argues that the economy works best when it is left alone by the government; he believed that the market operates according to the wishes and decisions of free individuals. Freedom within the market means freedom of choice—the ability of the businesses to choose what goods to make, the ability of workers to choose an employer, and the ability of consumers to choose what goods or services to buy. Relationships within such a market between employers and employees, between buyers and sellers, are thus based on voluntary and self-interested contracts. In this way, no single producer can set the price of commodity. Prices are set by the market, by the number of goods offered for sale, and by the number consumers are willing to buy; these are the forces of supply and demand, so the market is a self-regulating mechanism. The idea of a self-regulating market reflects the liberal belief in a naturally existing harmony amongst the conflicting interests within society. In this regard the market should be free from government interference because it is managed by what Adam Smith referred to as an "invisible hand". According to Adam Smith, it is not from the benevolence of the butcher, the brewer, or the baker that we expect our dinner, but from their regard to their own interests.

Unemployment, inflation, or budget deficit can be removed by the mechanisms of the market. Unemployment occurs when there are more people prepared to work than there are jobs available; when the government is unable to create new jobs, the supply of labour exceeds the demand. In these conditions, market forces push down the wages of labour. Because wages fall, businesses are able to recruit more workers, and unemployment drops. Employers are able to hire more workers because when wages fall, it increases the profits of business. Market forces can therefore lessen unemployment without the need of government interference.

However, by circumstance, liberals accept state intervention and argue that state intervention in the form of social welfare could extend liberty by safeguarding individuals from social problems. The liberals' commitment at this stage is to raise individuals to the point where they would be able to take responsibility for their own circumstances and make their own moral choices. Liberals advance the concept that the government should be responsible for delivering welfare services such as housing, health, and education. They believe that capitalism institution has led to new forms of social injustice.

5. Taxation, Free Market, and Regulation

5.1. Taxation

Why do countries introduce taxation in the free market? It is because countries' incomes come from taxes charged, and countries use taxes to pay the cost of services. Without a country's tax charges, the government would not be able to run services such as education. From this context, foreign investors are interested in doing business in Ireland because Ireland has an educated workforce. Thus multinational companies in Ireland are a result of the Irish-educated workforce. This means that tax charges are necessary to run the country's services. Lack of taxation results in the incapacity of the government to subsidize its industry and technology; in turn, this explains countries who are unsuccessful in the high-tech industry because successful the high-tech market is based on public subsidy. In this context, for example, the success of the US National Aeronautics and Space Administration could not happen without an American public subsidy. Furthermore, tax charges enforce behaviour; for example, raising off-licence tax charges could reduce drinking heavily because a tax raise on off-licence raises the price of alcohol. In a free market, every country decides the tax to be charged on businesses and on personal or household income.

Conservatives often argue that an increase in taxes harms businesses because the business tax reduces business profits, which in turn causes employment to fall. An increase in the business profits increases employment; however, tax charges are also necessary because they are used to educate people who increase profits in the business. In this regard, the government should consider low tax and flexible tax for businesses. Thus in the business, tax should increase according to the increase in their profits, but businesses should still pay low taxes. From this point, increasing profits in the business would also increase government revenues; in turn, this would advance country technology. which further increases public subsidy and the business profits. Technology expands business profits because it reduces the cost of making products.

Because the government raises taxes on employees' income when their income increases, it could be rational to consider a tax raise on businesses earning significant profits. However, because the effect of an increase in tax could harm businesses' and consumers' behaviour, taxation strategy should be based on economic conditions. In a period of economic downturn, low taxes would expand businesses while increasing consumption. However, policymakers should consider raising taxes on products that show a rise in prices. At this stage, the tax would not only reduce the likelihood of economic downturn, but it would also stabilise prices against inflation.

5.2. Free Market

In the early nineteenth century, economist David Ricardo demonstrated how free trade could be advantageous between two countries. According to his theory, he demonstrated that England could have an advantage by selling cloth to Portugal, and Portugal could have an advantage by selling wine in England. This suggestion of exchanging merchandise between England and Portugal was based on mutual advantage. From this context, countries could gain profits from the exchange of their products and create more jobs. In this respect, job creation could increase due to sustainable trade between countries, and this explains the probability to stop or reduce labour emigrating to other countries for employment. Free trade introduces a relationship in trade between nations, and every country could gain by specialising in the products where it has an advantage in comparative cost. Today, free trade is explained by comparative advantage, which itself is based on the export and import of products. Thus instead of a country producing products at high cost, it would have the advantage of importing those product at a lower cost from another country. In this context, despite a country exporting more products gaining more profits than a country importing products, both have an advantage to increase job creation. But in general, countries with lower costs to production have more advantage to sustain employment than countries with high cost to produce goods and services. Moreover, countries with more exports are considered competitive countries in trade, relative to countries that import products.

Free trade is still an important economic strategy between countries. It is not expressly a free market; it removes barriers in trade between countries, but trade barriers are removed according to a country's trade policy. Thus the import and export of goods are controlled by agreements between countries. In this context, for example, policy agreements of the European Free Trade Association (EFTA) are not the same as policy agreements of the Latin American Free Trade Area (LFTA) and the North American Free Trade Agreement (NAFTA).

Although free trade is regulated by a comparative advantage between countries, the free market is about freedom of business and consumers. Moreover, a free market allows consumers to choose what they want to consume—it allows individuals to develop their businesses without state intervention. Business owners choose the place where their investments will gain high profits. For example, in 2012 the French firm Renault opened a plant in Morocco to build cars in Morocco at a low cost. Opening the plant in Morocco did not mean that Renault abandoned production in France; however, labour costs in France is higher than labour in Morocco. In this regard, countries with free markets encourage competitiveness in the business, and competitiveness in the business not only creates jobs but also raises the profits of businesses while creating innovation.

In a free market, prices are set by demand, so every business sets prices according to consumer demand. Prices would be set at a high level if consumers increase their demand. Prices would also increase in periods of a shortage of goods caused by an expansion in the demand, a lack of resources, because of a natural disaster. In other words, market prices depend on consumer demand and the obtainability of goods in the markets.

5.3. Regulation

Well-functioning markets require informed sellers and buyers, and so market fail because of a lack of information in consumer choices. In this respect, governments may improve the information available to buyers. In the current debate, regulation has been subjected to the criticism that it harms free markets. However, regulation is necessary for businesses and community. Countries with well-functioning regulation reduce the cost in businesses while promoting innovation and competitiveness.

Conservatives state that the market can take care of itself without government intervention; moreover, they advance the idea that government regulation would make businesses worse. Despite the fact that regulations are there to control prices in the markets—and to reduce both corruption and fraud—regulations not only fail to counter monopolistic pricing, but they sustain monopoly pricing through state intervention. Furthermore, critics say that instead of promoting businesses, the government is promoting social welfare. Government regulation tends to promote wages to be given to the workers and social benefit to jobseekers, while it imposes a high tax to businesses.

In general, government regulation is about controlling prices in the market, so monopolies businesses do not overcharge or undercharge. Monopoly producers can overprice to earn economic rents—that is, excess profits. Moreover, buyers with monopoly power would be economically inefficient because they could drive rates below the marginal cost. In this context, perfect competition in the market is needed because it leads to economic efficiency. One producer does not have the market power to push prices above marginal cost. Additionally, buyers with a monopoly would not be able to push prices below the marginal cost.

In addition, government regulation imposes safety standards to prevent accidents in the workplace. In this respect, injured employees can sue their employers for damages. To prevent employees from being abused by employers, the government regulates employers' power. Additionally, with regulation, the government could produce information to help financial institutions against fraud or corruption in the markets. In this context, investors can sue issuers and underwriters for damages if they believe that representations about the company's prospects were false or incomplete. So although government regulation solves social problems, it also imposes discipline in the free markets.

Conservatives prefer deregulation of the markets as a means of solving social problems while sustaining businesses. However, the 2008 recession indicated that businesses and financial institutions cannot only self-sustain, but they also cannot cure businesses which are in a situation of failure. Government regulation is necessary because they sustain the positive effects of the rule of laws in financial institutions. Although it may reduce businesses' output directly, such as environmental regulation, it facilitates indirect, positive economic effects, such as through an improvement in public health.

Government regulation cannot work if businesses and financial institutions do not wish to provide palpable information to regulators. The reasons that can cause financial institutions and business to provide wrong information could be fraud or corruption within their services. At this stage, fraud and corruption not only misallocate investment, but they make businesses unsustainable. Socialists advance the idea that markets are unsustainable because of a deregulation of the markets. However, the problem is not the markets being free markets—the problem is a fraud and corruption that misallocates investment. In this condition, both financial institutions and regulators need to be incorrupt to be able to regulate corruption and fraud in the markets. Thus, free markets are sustainable when they are free from fraud and corruption that misallocates capital. In this context, free markets work efficiently when both buyers and sellers are well informed. In markets when the buyers may be more informed than the seller, and vice versa, the markets become inefficient. For example, in insurance markets, buyers know more than sellers. As an outcome, only buyers with higher risks will tend to purchase more insurance because they are more certain that the benefit of the insurance will exceed the cost; this could cause an increase in the price of insurance. At this stage, it is necessary for government regulators to provide information to the uninformed party. In this respect, the government would move the market back to an efficient outcome.

Furthermore, the financial sector also needs regulation because, for example, the manager of a bank may not have the same incentives as the depositors regarding the costs of risk-taking. In this regard, information disclosure and the implementation of accounting laws would maintain the behaviour of bank managers. Thus governments could improve businesses through regulation. Although regulation is needed in business, low-quality regulation increases the cost of business. Regulations can reduce competitiveness in the business; for example, regulations can prevent businesses from competing by setting rules that reduce business profitability. In this context, although taxation is needed to run country services, high taxation reduces the profitability of business. Furthermore, regulation could often cause consumers to change their behaviour. If regulation results in an increase in the price of goods, consumers will respond by purchasing less of those goods and switching to substitute goods. Regulations work well when they are there to support businesses rather than to serve one group's interests. In the political arena, regulation denotes Keynesian economics, whereas a free market denotes classical economics.

CHAPTER IV

▼

European Union—Origins and Solutions to Unemployment

Without understanding the origins of the European Union, it is difficult to understand the objectives of the EU in relation to European Union Economic Integration and to the reason that motivated the European leaders, particularly France and Germany, to introduce the Fiscal Treaty. This chapter takes the reader through the origins of the European Union and the policies pursued by European Union in relation to unemployment, as well as the main reason that pushed Eurozone leaders to introduce the European Fiscal Treaty.

1. The Origins of the European Union[8]

The origins of the European Union stem from the failure of the main countries of Europe in the early post-war period to reach an agreement regarding how to proceed towards European unity. France and West Germany formed an alliance to promote European integration, to rebuild their shattered economic systems, and to foster the conditions that would prevent war between Western European countries. This alliance gave the Franco-Germany union a major role in defining and developing the European Union. Italy, Belgium, Holland, and Luxembourg supported the Franco-Germany alliance, and these six countries started the process that ultimately led to the European

---

[8]   See El-Agraa A. M. (2007), *The European Union: Economics and Policies, Eighth Edition,* Cambridge University Press.

Union. In the United Kingdom and the Scandinavian countries, the predominant view was that inter-governmental approach should be taken to rebuild Europe and to secure stability in the region.

These early developments in the European Unit movement have had long-lasting effects. The Franco-Germany alliance came to dominate the process of European integration because its view tended to regard European unity as primarily a political issue, and economic considerations were a means to a political end. This end was seen as being primarily the creation of security and prosperity by integration, and economic efficiency considerations were secondary to the goal of achieving unit. The importance of this view can perhaps be best observed in the creation of such policies as the Common Agricultural Policy (CAP), which is very strong on stability, security, and the prosperity of farmers, but it had little connection with the concept of economic efficiency.

The European Union has developed largely in accordance with the vision of the Franco-Germany alliance, which tended to guide the development of the community—but this has led to resistance by Italy and the smaller member states, who have sought to curb the power of the alliance by increasing the supranational aspects of the community. The scepticism of the United Kingdom and the Scandinavians towards plans for greater political integration and the extension of supranationalism stems in part from their different perception of the purpose of the European Union. However, they have not been able to steer the community away from the powerful influence of the Franco-Germany alliance.

The differences within the European Union can be seen in attitudes towards European monetary union. The Franco-Germany alliance regards monetary union largely as a political imperative to weld the countries of the community together while allowing the alliance to continue to drive developments. Italy and smaller member states regard it as a means to lessen the power of Germany in monetary matters. The United Kingdom and the Scandinavians tend to regard the project in a more pragmatic light, considering it to be a potentially beneficial move for some, but not necessarily all, of the member states. However, they also regard monetary union as raising very serious questions about the sovereignty of member states.

In the 1950s, matters relating to foreign relations and military arrangements were heavily influenced by the development of the Cold War. The dominance of the United States of America and the Soviet Union in security and military matters resulted in setting up opposing alliances in Europe—the Warsaw Pact in Eastern Europe, and the North Atlantic Treaty Organisation (NATO) in Western Europe. The former institution was dominated by the Soviet Union, and the latter by the United States of America. The early attempts to establish economic and non-military political arrangements in Western Europe were centred on the Organisation for European Economic Cooperation (OEEC) and the Council of Europe. The OEEC failed to develop because of disputes about the need for some kind of supranational decision-making power. It eventually expanded its membership and became the Organisation for Economic Cooperation and Development (OECD). The council of Europe was not granted any supranational powers and still exists as a forum for inter-governmental discussion on issues of interest for Europe, America, and other countries.

By the early 1950s, a series of inter-governmental agencies existed in Western Europe: the Council of Europe, the OEEC, and NATO. For those countries that favoured more supranational powers for European agencies, these institutions did not seem to be capable of integrating Europe. In 1948, Belgium, Luxembourg, and the Netherlands agreed to form a Customs Union (CU). This example of the use of specific economic means of achieving European union was to come to foreground in the development of community. The main political and military issues in Western Europe were heavily influenced by NATO and the Americans and were firmly based on inter-governmentalism; the European Federalists and Functionalists were therefore unable to expand their ideas into these matters. In the immediate post-war period, there was popular opposition within Western Europe to allowing Germany any such role in these areas. Consequently, the Federalists and the Functionalists were restricted to economic matters in proposals for any supranational agency.

In those countries where Federalist and Functionalist views were strong (France, Germany, Italy, Holland, Belgium, and Luxembourg; the original six), there was a desire to establish agencies with some supranational powers, and this led them to establish the European Coal and Steel Community (ECSC) in 1951. One of the motives for this community was to integrate the coal and steel industries of Germany, the heart of its war machine, into an interdependent European industrial structure—thereby making war between Western European countries impossible. The European Coal and Steel Community had a high authority that had some supranational powers in the areas of coal and steel, but the main decision-making powers rested with the Council of Ministers. The council was composed of the ministers of the member states and was therefore inter-governmental in character. Nevertheless, the ECSC was an agency that had some supranational powers and was a kind of cross between an inter-governmental and a supranational agency. This mixture was also to characterise the European Economic Community (EEC) and the European Atomic Energy (EURATOM) community, the agencies that followed the ECSC and from which the European Union (EU) raised. Consequently, the origins of the EU led to an institutional structure that was focused on economic matters and was neither a pure inter-governmental nor a supranational agency, but rather a mixture of these forms.

The setup of the EEC and the EURATOM resulted from the Spaak Committee.[9] The United Kingdom joined with the original six countries represented on this committee, but the UK withdrew when it became clear that they wanted new institutional forms based on the ECSC model and were also seeking wide-ranging economic integration. The United Kingdom did not join the original six when they established the EEC and EURATOM by the Treaty of Roma, signed in 1957. Instead, the United Kingdom formed the European Free Trade Association (EFTA) in 1960 with Austria, Switzerland, Norway, Sweden, Denmark, and Portugal. The arrangements with EFTA were considerably less ambitious than the EEC. The EEC had elements of supranationality in decision-making and was committed to the establishment of a Customs Union and Common Market, and it had vaguely defined objectives to

---

[9]   See Spaak, P. (1956), *Intergovernmental Committee on European Integration*.

create the Economic and Monetary Union (EMU), whereas EFTA was purely inter-governmental and was aiming to achieve a free-trade area.

By the early 1960s, Europe appeared to have created a new political order based on the division of Europe into East and West (with the Soviet Union and the United States largely directing events in this area), and an economic order based on the EEC, the EFTA, and the Council for Mutual Economic Assistance. However, the EEC was soon to emerge as the dominant economic agency in Europe.

During the 1970s and early 1980s, the integration process did not progress until the deadlock was broken by the agreement on the Single European Act (SEA), and this led to the Maastricht Treaty and the preparation for EMU. The aims of the Single European Act included a commitment to the harmonisation of national provisions in regard to health, safety, and environmental and consumer protection (Articles 100a, 118a), and to policies fostering "the economic and social cohesion of community" (Articles 130a-130e). Article 118b committed the community to the encouragement of a "social dialogue" between management and labour. By the early 1990s, the community had made considerable progress in establishing the Single European Market (SEM); it had also developed detailed plans for the creation of monetary union, and there was a growing momentum to increase community competencies in the social, environmental, and regional areas. Moreover, the reunification of Germany and the collapse of communism in the Eastern Europe countries (CEECS) swept away the post-war economic and political order of Europe. These factors led to pressure to increase the integration programmes of the community. Germany and France in particular sought to deepen the integration of the community. To achieve these aims, the community established two Inter-Governmental Conferences (IGCs), one on economic and monetary union and one on political union. The IGCs led to the negotiations on the Maastricht Treaty, also known as the Treaty on European Union (TEU). As the first treaty on European Union, the Maastricht Treaty was negotiated, and after three years the Single European Act legally came into force: it was signed in December 1991 in Maastricht (Holland). The Maastricht Treaty went into force on 1 November 1993 and signifies a greater departure from the original EEC treaty. Thus in the Maastricht Treaty, economic aims are reformulated and extended. However, after the Maastricht Treaty the EU struggled to cope with the problem of high unemployment.

2. Tackling Unemployment in the European Union

During the 1980s unemployment increased across Europe, and there was persistence unemployment in the 1990s. In this regard, in 1992at the Edinburgh meeting, the European Council put forward an initiative to coordinate macroeconomic policies to help boost non-inflationary growth in the European Union. This initiative was meant to lower unemployment. In 1993 the commission published a White Paper on *Growth, Competitiveness and Employment* (European Commission, 1993). The White Paper set a target of fifteen million new jobs in the European Union by the year 2000. To achieve this target, the member countries were encouraged to pursue policies that would deliver non-inflationary growth, create more jobs from growth, and improve the global competitiveness of European-based companies.

In order to ensure that the growth was non-inflationary, the White Paper argued that the member states should not expand their public-sector deficits. Moreover, the European Commission encouraged fast-growing industries such as information technology, telecommunications services and equipment, and biotechnology. In addition, it recommended that steps should be taken to avoid the creation of large numbers of low-paid and low-skilled jobs. But the White Paper advocated that part-time working should be encouraged and that work sharing might contribute to find ways to lower the unemployment rate. The commission also recommended the use of government help to lower the costs to companies of hiring the long-term unemployed and young people. It argued that unemployment was the major economic problem facing the European Union.

The recovery began in 1994 but lost its way in 1995. Unemployment averaged 10.7 per cent in 1996, only slightly below its peak of 11.3 per cent in April 1994, and long-term unemployed composed half of the total. More jobs created in the 1990s have been part-time, with 71 per cent of additional male employment being part-time in 1995 and 85 per cent for women. Similarly, almost all of the increase in employment for men was on temporary contracts, and just under half of that for women (European Commission, 1996b).

The unemployment problem was on the top of the agenda at the Essen Summit in December 1994. Five priorities had been identified.

1. Promoting investment in vocational training
2. Increasing employment and the intensiveness of growth
3. Reducing non-wage labour costs
4. Improving the effectiveness of labour market policies
5. Helping disadvantaged groups

At the Essen Summit, the commission convened to examine the impact of social security contributions on employment. In 1995 the commission addressed job creation in its recommendations on economic policy for the community (COM[95] 228). Even though the recommendation did not indicate real evidence of policy convergence among national employment policies, the Essen Summit encouraged the movement to fiscal harmonisation. A commission paper (SEC[96] 487) had observed that between 1980 and 1994, the implicit tax rate on employed labour had grown by 14 per cent, while that of other factors of production had fallen by 20 per cent. This is incompatible with the desired objective of increasing employment through reducing indirect labour costs.

In 1997, the commission's president, Jacques Santer, proposed a Confidence Pact on Employment that focused on policies including the adoption of coordinated macro-economic policies favourable to employment creation, policies to encourage job creation in small—and medium-sized enterprises, and realising the potential of the internal market as well as redirecting structural funds towards employment objectives. Furthermore, the Amsterdam Treaty required the council to monitor employment conditions in the states and to make proposals that would help to reduce unemployment. The treaty did not envisage that large-scale legislation or new European Union policies would be generated by this procedure; rather it predicted that information on what was happening in the member states would be shared to help national governments to craft their own responses to their unemployment problems (Duff, 1997).

In addition to the Luxembourg summit discussions in 1997, the European Employment Strategy was again on the agenda in 2000 at the Lisbon European Council. There was a desire to focus on retraining and mobility in order to address the emerging skills gaps in regional labour markets.

3. Vocational Training

Ensuring provisions for the training of the labour force was seen as essential to achieve the structural adjustment necessary for successful completion of single European markets. The commission sought to develop a strategy building upon discussions with both sides of industry, focusing on the training of young people, and building upon a council decision (December 1987) calling for the setting up of a system giving all young people the right to up to two years "basic training". In addition, the commission sought to improve comparability between national training systems as well as foster recognition of the importance of continuing training of the labour force by both industry and state.

On the basis of the White Paper *Growth, Competition and Employment* (COM [93] 700), the commission presented another White Paper, *Teaching and Learning: Towards the Learning Society* (COM [95] 590), which attempted to identify the response that was necessary to meet the challenges presented by globalisation and technological change. It considered the central role of education and training, and it called for recognition of the benefits of broad-based knowledge and training that was relevant to employment. It recommended the establishment of a network of European Union research centres to identify skill shortages, and vocational training centres to meet this need.

In relation to higher education, it sought to enhance mobility through ensuring the portability between member states of education grants and the mutual recognition of course credits through a European Course Credit Transfers Scheme. To address the problem of "school failures" (concentrated in the community's decaying urban centres), the commission proposed redeploying funds to support national "second chance" schemes targeted at these groups. Additionally, the commission called for the equal treatment of investment in physical and human capital in taxation and accounting terms.

At the European Council of Lisbon (2000), there was a new emphasis to a coherent approach towards economic development, social cohesion, and employment. Member countries committed themselves to the principal of social policy, including achieving full employment, improving the quality of work and productivity, making labour markets more accessible, placing greater emphasis upon education and training, increasing employment in services as well as promoting equal opportunities, and guaranteeing efficient social policies. To achieve these commitments, the European Union adopted Broad Economic Policy Guidelines (BEPG), which makes both general and country-specific recommendations, identifying the key economic policy areas which will contribute to economic stability and structural reforms. In the beginning of 2003 the BEPGS have been published simultaneously with the employment guidelines and recommendations; these BEPGS complement the Stability and Growth Pact (SGP), which is intended to provide the national fiscal discipline necessary to underpin European Monetary Union. It involves the submission of member states' stability and convergence programmes to the council for collective assessment and a commitment to the medium-term objective of balanced government budgets, while allowing some flexibility during the economic cycles as long as the deficit does not exceed 3 per cent of gross domestic product. If the deficit is a result of "exceptional circumstances" beyond the control of the member countries, or a result of a severe economic recession, then no further action will be taken. At this stage, the countries will face the possibility of the council imposing sanctions. The sanctions take the form of non-interest-bearing deposits with the commission equal to 0.2 per cent of GDP plus an element linked to the size of the deficit, up to a total maximum of 0.5 per cent of GDP. If after two years the excessive deficit has not been corrected, then the deposit becomes a permanent fine distributed to the other member countries.

However, both Germany and France were exceeding the deficit limit and received no sanctions. A lack of sanction to both France and Germany has raised question about the credibility of the Stability and Growth Pact (SGP). It is from this context that Germany and France proposed the European Fiscal Treaty, which contains obligated rules in relation to Eurozone states' deficit limit. At this stage, because the SGP is incorporated in the European Fiscal Treaty, it will significantly reduce the risk that the rules will be neglected as they were in years prior. European member states who accepted to ratify the European Fiscal Treaty would not alter the treaty rules without going through institutional procedures that would involve constitutional amendment. Moreover, although the fiscal treaty is designed to "compel" loan recipient states to maintain austerity measures in order to ensure that the creditor states will be repaid, the Fiscal Treaty includes a clause that explains that only states that have ratified the treaty will be able to request emergency funding from the European Stabilisation Mechanism (ESM). At this point, it was and is necessary for Greece, Ireland, and Italy to ratify the fiscal treaty if they think that they could need emergency loan disbursements from the Euro area's monetary fund.

4. The European Union Fiscal Treaty

Because of the debt crisis and fiscal crisis in the Eurozone countries from 2008, the European Union decided to establish the European Financial Stability Facility (EFSF) to channel loans from Eurozone states to other Eurozone countries faced with a severe balance of payment. The EFSF was established on 9 May 2010, and it has been activated for Ireland in 2010 and for Portugal in 2011.

However, since the European Court of Justice could declare the loans from EFSF to be illegal under European Treaty Law, and could therefore invoke those loans, Germany and France proposed a treaty change, and both countries agreed on the need to ensure repayment on their loans channelled through the EFSF by "compelling" Eurozone countries receiving such loans to implement austerity measures to ensure debt sustainability. In this way, in 2010 at the "Deauville Declaration", German and French Leaders called for an amendment of treaties on the basis of establishing a permanent framework to ensure orderly crisis management in the future, and to allow member states to adopt coordinated measures to safeguard the financial stability of the Eurozone. The amendment also allowed for the suspension of a member state's voting rights in the council of ministers, in case of a serious violation of basic principles of economic and monetary union. The two leaders reiterated that the necessary amendment to the treaties should be adopted and ratified by member states in accordance with their respective constitutional requirement in due time, before 2013. At this stage, all European member states had adopted a decision to amend Article 136 of the Treaty on the Functioning of the European Union (TFEU), which concerns governance of the Euro areas to provide a firm legal basis for the European Stabilization Mechanism (ESM). Even though all European Member States are required to ratify this treaty amendment, in practice Article 136 will apply only to Euro area states. Because the United Kingdom vetoed against the European Union treaty revision procedures and the fiscal treaty, Germany proposed that the amendments would be enacted with a special emphasis on participation by Euro area states. In this context, the Stability and Growth Pact would hold the status of treaty law while allowing the United Kingdom to remain unaffected by the new rules. In this respect, according to article 4(3) of the Treaty on European Union, the fiscal treaty expressly states that is complies with the European Union's "duty of loyal cooperation". This clause requires all European member states not to undermine the operation of European treaty rules and to respect the rights of the European Union institutions in implementing the rules. In this regard, though ratification of the fiscal treaty is an obligation to Eurozone states, it is regarded as voluntary to non-Eurozone states. Moreover, the treaty requires a minimum number of twelve states to ratify before it can enter into force, even though the target is for all Eurozone states to ratify the treaty. Critics argue that although member states that ratify the treaty will lose sovereignty over their own budgetary process, they will remain fully sovereign over their own budget, but they are obliged under the fiscal treaty to share information and, if necessary, accept proposed alterations to national debt reduction plans from other member states or the commission.

The three key elements in the fiscal treaty include the following.

1. The establishment of a "golden rule" to ensure budgetary discipline.
2. The policing of national budgetary control at a supranational level through a stricter, excessive deficit procedure, including legal penalties and control by the European Court of Justice.
3. New institutional architecture for Euro area governance.

The golden rules reinforce stability and growth pact, as well as the stricter excessive deficit rules that are already in place. It is at the heart of the fiscal treaty and stipulates that a general government's structural should not be greater than 0.5 per cent for countries that have a debt-to-GDP ratio of over 60 per cent, and not greater than 1.0 per cent for countries whose debt is below the 60 per cent ratio. The golden rule is accompanied by other rules: these rules are a 60 per cent general government debt-to-GDP ratio and a 3 per cent annual government deficit-to-GDP ratio. Moreover, the countries that ratify the fiscal treaty are required to reduce their debt-to-GDP ratio by one-twentieth of the difference between their present debt-to-GDP ratio and the 60 per cent target every year. But the fiscal treaty allows states to deviate its contents in case of severe economic downturn caused by exceptional circumstances or unusual events outside the state's control. At this stage, in addition to natural disaster, it would be better if Eurozone governments determine what are exceptional circumstances or unusual events outside state control.

Table 5 shows that the majority of states are currently not compliant with the golden rule.

Table 5

	General government debt % of GDP Target: 60%	General government deficit % of GDP Target: -3%	Structural deficit % of GDP Target: 0.5%
EU countries			
Austria	71.8	-4.4	-3.7
Belgium	96.2	-4.1	-2.9
Cyprus	61.5	-5.3	-5.1
Estonia	6.7	0.2	-0.4
Finland	48.3	-2.5	0.3
France	82.3	-7.1	-4.9
Germany	83.2	-4.3	-1.9
Greece	144.9	-10.6	-8.6
Ireland	92.5	-31.3	-10.5
Italy	118.4	-4.6	-3.1
Luxembourg	19.1	-1.1	0.1
Malta	69.0	-3.6	-4.6
Holland	62.9	-5.1	-3.7
Portugal	93.3	-9.8	-9.2
Slovakia	41.0	-7.7	-7.3
Slovenia	38.0	-5.8	-3.0
Spain	61.0	-9.3	-7.0
Non-Eurozone Countries			
Bulgaria	16.3	-3.1	-1.3
Czech Republic	37.6	-4.8	-4.1
Denmark	43.7	-2.6	0.2
Hungary	81.3	-4.2	-3.1
Latvia	44.7	-8.3	-3.7
Lithuania	38.0	-7.0	-5.7
Poland	54.9	-7.8	-7.4
Romania	31.0	-6.9	-5.5
Sweden	39.9	0.2	1.4
United Kingdom	79.9	-10.3	-8.2

Source: *Eurostat Commission, Autumn 2011, European Economic Forecast*

The states that ratify the fiscal treaty are required to begin reducing their structural deficit to converge to a medium-term objective (MTO) of 0.35 per cent by 2016. In general the main reason that pushed French and German leaders to propose an introduction of the fiscal treaty was the need for members of European state governments to maintain sound and sustainable government fiscal policy, to prevent a budget deficit in the Eurozone areas. After experiencing the 2008 fiscal crisis in the Eurozone states, Eurozone governments introduce the fiscal treaty, whose contents imposed the Eurozone governments to apply the rules preventing future fiscal crisis in the Eurozone countries. In this context, however, preventing fiscal crisis would be difficult if the Eurozone states did not reform their rules in relation to Eurozone's external states policy. In other words, sustainable Eurozone economic integration needs Eurozone states' law reform in relation to internal and external policy. Fiscal treaty is not enough to cut Eurozone governments' expenditure. In addition to fiscal treaty, tough regulations are needed for cutting and ceiling Eurozone governments' expenditures. Otherwise the Eurozone economy will continue to weaken due to unnecessary expenditures.

Notes

Addison J. and Siebert W. S. (1997), *Labour Markets in Europe: Issues of Harmonisation and Regulation*, Dryden Press, London.

Duff A. (1997), *The Treaty of Amsterdam*, Sweet & Maxwell/Federal Trust, London.

O Broin P. (2012), *The Euro Crisis: The Fiscal Treaty—An Initial Analysis*, Working Paper, No 5, Institute of International and European Affairs, Dublin.

European Commission (1993), *White Paper on Growth, Competitiveness and Employment*, COM (93) 700 Final, Brussels.

European Commission (1997), *Agenda 2000: For a Stronger and Wider Union*, Communication from the Commission to the Council and the EP, COM (97) 2000, Brussels.

Nugent N. (2003), *The Government and Politics of the European Community*, Palgrave, Basingstoke.

European Commission (1996b), *Employment in Europe*, Brussels.

CHAPTER V

▼

European Union Economic Integration (EUEI) and Practice

1. Economic Integration

Economic integration is an arrangement between different countries or regions dedicated to the reduction or removal of trade barriers and the coordination of monetary and fiscal policies. The goal of economic integration is therefore to reduce costs for both consumers and businesses. In this context, when states linked by economic integration, they are said to have formed a free-trade area, which is also known as a single common market. In addition to free-trade area, a common market allows free movement of labour and capital among member states. In this respect, therefore, economic integration occurs when a group of states in the region are relatively equal in their stages of development, and they join together to form customs union and common external tariffs on the goods and services of non-member states. However, since the enlargement of the European Union in 2004, the European Union member states are not relatively equal at their stages of development. This explains why new member states need radical changes in their policy system in order to implement the relative stage of development the European Union needs.

In practice, economic integration needs to be viewed as a mechanism to encourage a free movement of labour and investors among member states, and as a result each member state would benefit from such a movement by itself. In this context, however, the making of a sustainable

European Union Economic Integration (EUEI) should not only be an integrated free movement of labour, goods, services, and investors, but also a strong regional policy in relation to the integration of member states with high unemployment and low standards of living. In other words, although the European member states are becoming increasingly integrated with economies based on trade links and free capital mobility and labour, the member states with unsustainable economies need a sustainable policy for job creation instead of depending on member states with sustainable economies and high standards of living.

Even though the Eurozone states' commitment is ensuring a fair standard of living and the reduction of unemployment in the Eurozone states, if some states in the Eurozone are not self-sustained in order to solve their problems of high unemployment, then this will compromise the economic integration in Eurozone states. Thus if some states could not create sustainable jobs, it will jeopardise Eurozone Economic Integration because the dependent states will cause an increase in welfare spending in Eurozone states, which further will cause budget deficit that itself depresses economic growth.

In addition to the work of the Commission of European Union in relation to European Union Economic Integration, some member states of the European Union need to find their own way of joining in the European Union Economic Integration. In other words, the economic integration in the European Union needs to be analysed and considered in a dynamic context of member states' economic growth and current member states' economic integration policies, rather than in the theoretical traditional common market.

2. European Union Governments on Job Creation

Can EU governments create strategies which can sustain employment and job creation? In economic terms, job creation has traditionally been based on the planned alternation of the structure of production so that while employment in agriculture declines, employment in manufacturing and services industries increases. From this way, therefore, job creation strategy was continually based on industrialisation and services such as education, health, and construction services. Moreover, employment was progressively sustained by businesses capital gain—in other words, job creation was progressively sustained by private sectors. Similar to the traditional strategy of job creation, nowadays job creation is continually based on a strategy of creating manufacturing which produces new products, such as computers and software. Job creation is also mainly sustained by the private sector rather than the public sector. In this context from the 1990s, the Republic of Ireland experienced increased job creation within the private sector from both the information technology and pharmaceutical sectors, as well as in construction services. However, since 2008 Ireland has experienced a decline in employment and job creation. But not only the Republic of Ireland experienced a decline in employment from 2008; countries in Europe such as Greece, Italy, Spain, and Portugal experienced a decline in employment as well. Moreover, the problem of decline in employment and job creation is not only experienced by the European Union but also by North America and other continents.

Some Irish politicians attributed the Irish decline in employment and job creation to the 2008 international recession, whereas others argue that it was caused by bank deregulation and excessive government expenditure. In this regard the European Union countries, and particularly Eurozone member states, continue to create strategies which can prevent a decline in employment and job creation in Eurozone while creating favourable conditions for employment in the European Union. At this stage, however, anyone who experienced the current recession in Ireland can suggest that it is impossible that EU governments can create strategies which can bring back sustainable, favourable conditions for job creation in the Eurozone and in the European Union. Responses on this suggestion as to whether European Union can create an environment which would cause permanent, favourable conditions for employment and job creation can come from the EU governance board dedicated to sustainable job creation.

In fact, because governance is a fundamental source of job creation, this means that Eurozone states will sustain job creation with good governance, while Eurozone states with bad governance will be unable to sustain employment. In this context, therefore, ineffective government compromises the ability of a country to succeed in the management of job creation, while effective governments succeed in implementing principles of job creation. In this way, because governments are legally responsible for every decision in relation to a country's management, effective governments in the Eurozone and in the European Union will be able to sustain favourable conditions for job creation, while ineffective governments will not. The European Union governance board will be able to sustain employment in the European Union if its rules that impose its governments' member states to be effective are respected and implemented.

3. Tackling Young Graduate Unemployment

Young graduate unemployment is increasing across all European Union countries since the 2008 economic crisis. Until now there have been no pragmatic responses from governments to tackle this unemployment. Only a training programme is the key for resolving the problem of unemployment. However, it is impossible to resolve unemployment without understanding the present state of employment. The 2008 recession changed the nature of available jobs. Consequently, since 2008 the housing market—which was a key stimulant of job creation in the member of European Union—is in decline. Moreover, all types of businesses and services are also in decline. Because unequal distribution of the wealth had been created by the 1990s economic growth, the result was a decline of services in many sectors from 2008 onwards. In other words, because the majority of populations lacked purchasing power in the market, many sectors made redundancies with their workers and they stopped hiring new workers. Additionally, although many think that an increase in the rate of unemployment for young graduates is a result of the 2008 recession, it is actually a result of the absence of creation of enough skilled jobs during economic growth. Thus during the last period of economic growth, there was not enough creation of skilled jobs; instead, there were jobs for unskilled and semi-skilled workers.

Resolving the problem of young graduates needs pragmatic responses. Although the European Union governments encourage young graduates to create their own opportunities, every EU government needs to set up a management board dedicated to organising the training of unemployed young graduates according to their specific professional choices. This means that instead of mismatching aspirations of young graduates, it is better to set up a management board dedicated to fulfil their professional choices during their studies. In this respect the young graduates can change their professional choice if they wish to be more flexible in labour market.

Today more jobs in Western countries are created by innovation that resulted from new governments' strategy for sustaining employment or from new businesses' strategy for increasing profits. In this respect innovations are derived from both human aspirations and human expectations. Governments need not mismatch the aspirations and expectations of young graduates in order to succeed in innovation. In this context, to tackle unemployment in the young graduates, the Commission of European Union has already set up a traineeships office which is organised in two terms; summer traineeship and winter traineeship. The training from the Commission of European Union is to give university graduates the opportunity to put in practice their knowledge and to introduce them into the working environment in order to gain experience in their choice of profession. Moreover, the training provides an understanding of the objectives and goals of the European Union's integration process and policies. In this way, if every government in the European Union tackles the problem of unemployment of university graduates in the same way as the Commission of European Union does, the rate in unemployment for university graduates could decline. In other words, while the Commission of European Union is dedicated for training that provides an understanding of the European Union goals, every state member of European Union can commit to training their own graduates. In this direction, every European state needs to create an environment which can help young graduates practice their experience from training.

A management board dedicated to university graduate employment can be effective if its composition is located in the university and the private sectors.

4.   Tackling Youth Unemployment

Statistics and numerous quantitative studies of the sources of economic growth indicated that it was not the growth of physical capital but rather of human capital that was the principal source of economic progress in developed nations.[10] Moreover, According to Frederick H. Harbison,

> Human resources constitute the ultimate basis for the wealth of nations. Capital and natural resources are passive factors of production; human beings are the active agents who accumulate capital, exploit natural resources, build social, economic and political organisations, and carry forward national development. Clearly, a country which is unable to develop the skills and knowledge of its people and to utilise them effectively in the national economy will be unable to develop anything else.[11]

In above context, while it is not the natural resources of a nation that first determines job creation, many economists would certainly agree that it is the human resources of a nation that firstly determine the path of its economic growth and social development, which itself can create jobs while sustaining employment.

---

[10]   See Edward Denison, *The Sources of Economic Growth in the United States* (New York: National Bureau of Economic Research, 1962), and Robert Solow, "Technical Change and the Aggregate Production Function", *Review of Economics and Statistics* (August 1957).

[11]   See Frederick H. Harbison, *Human Resources as the Wealth of Nations* (New York: Oxford University Press, 1973), p.3. See also Theodore W. Schultz, "Investment in Human Capital", *American Economic Review* 51 (March 1961).

Today the phenomena of persistently high rates of youth unemployment are largely structured in nature to the decline in education and training of youth. In this context, in addition to laying off workers, the 2008 economic crisis most heavily affected the unskilled and semi-skilled youth. According to the Organisation for Economic Co-operation and Development's "Employment Outlook 2011",

> Youth were hit disproportionately hard by the recession. In the first quarter of 2011, the unemployment rate for young people (aged 15 to 24) was 17.4 per cent in the OECD area compared with 7 per cent for adults (aged 25 and over). Youth who are neither in employment nor in education or training are a group at high risk of marginalisation and exclusion from the labour market, especially the longer they remain outside the world of work. Investing in youth and giving them a better start in the world of work should be a key policy objective. Otherwise, there is a high risk of persistence or growth in the hard-core group of youth who are left behind, facing poor employment and earnings prospects.[12]

Even though there are many services dedicated to training the unemployed, the problem of youth unemployment needs both specific programmes to be introduced and specific institutions to be able to help and use effectively youths in the working environment. Similar to strategies to reduce the number unemployed young graduates, one specific programme would be to reduce youth employment by encouraging them in training. However, it would be better if youth training could be based on their professional aspirations. In other words, both semi-skilled and unskilled youth can be trained according to their interests, in relation to employment. In this way, youth training needs to be organised in both the short run and the long run. In practice, this means that short-term training should only be based on available employment, whereas long-term training should be considered on the basis of employment opportunities. At this stage, because a lack of information about employment opportunities retards job creation,

---

[12] Organisation for Economic Co-operation and Development, "Employment Outlook 2011".

management institutions of employment need to gather information about employment opportunities. In this context, updated labour market information between EU member states would save time for European Union policymakers for making decisions on job creation. Moreover, knowing employment opportunities not only reduces government expenditure, but it increases government savings for future employment, which would be created by human training. Additionally, based on updates of labour market information, governments can increase savings in research of future employment.

Productive Training

The objective of formal education and training is to increase human skills, which creates and increases the production of goods and services. The rise in the production of goods and services in turn increases job creation; and there is an increase in employment for the distribution of those goods and services. In this process, while the objective of formal education and training in the long run are organised on the basis of human expectations of the current and future employment or future working environment, training in the short term needs to be organised by considering the current employment and the number of employees needed in the present working environment. The training outnumber of the number of employees needed in the current employment could be identified as investing in the housing markets without buyers of houses. Many houses are unsold because they were built without considering the state of current employment of people who would like to buy a house. In other words, unsold houses are the result of a lack of jobs for people who would like to buy a home. In this context, I view government expenditures on short-term training, without considering employment opportunities, as **unproductive expenditures**.

For example, my friend is formally trained in computer software development. But because he is now beyond one year without acquiring a job in his field, he said to me that he would like to have training if he got the chance to find employment. Moreover, I have a friend who was trained in the European Computer Driving Licence (ECDL), but he never found employment; he also said to me that if he got the chance to work, he would like to be trained before he started work. These two examples explain how government spending in short-term training becomes an unproductive investment. In other words, if the government spent on training without considering the number of employees needed in the current employment field, additional training will be unproductive because of a lack of employment. Furthermore, the government will spend more to retrain those who are already trained. In this way, because of the government's lack of information about labour markets, its expenditures in the short run training will increase without a benefit return. Government spending in unproductive training will result in government budget deficit because of the lack of employment, which caused the government revenue to rise.

Workers need training or retraining because:

1. Currently there are no jobs available.
2. Workers are qualified for jobs available; however, they want to learn further skills.
3. The jobs available do not perfectly match the skills for the unemployed.

Although the second category is the workers who need to learn more skills, the third category could be identified as new graduates who need more training. New graduates need further training because their qualifications are difficult to match with the jobs available. For example, a graduate qualified as a primary school teacher cannot work in the banking sector. In this regard, this graduate with a qualification of teaching needs further training to match his or her interests with the available jobs, and this training would be long-term training.

5.   Reducing Government Deficit

To attempt to reduce government deficits, it is necessary first to know the source of the government revenue and government sector expenditures.

Government Revenue Sources

1. Taxes on Income

Taxes on income are the personal income tax and corporation tax, which is a tax on profits. At this stage, tax cuts reduce government revenue, while a rise in taxes increases government revenue.

2. Taxes on Expenditures

Taxes on expenditures include all taxes on goods and services that people buy. Value-added taxes (VATs) have the highest yield, followed by taxes from oil and alcohol and tobacco. Other taxes in this category include property tax, tax on cars, tariffs on imports, and public charges. Low taxes on expenditures reduce government revenue.

3. Other Sources of Government Revenue

Other government revenue comes from government loans to businesses and from the sales of both nationalized industries and government housing.

Government Sector Expenditures

1. Expenditure on Goods and Services

The government sector's expenditure on goods and services covers the cost of services provided. In this way, the government spends its income on public services such as education and health, public infrastructure, research and development, innovation, social protection, social welfare, social housing, community amenities, and leisure and recreational facilities, as well as on military and police.

2. Government Subsidies for Business

Subsidies are benefits in the form of a cash payment or tax reduction given by the government to individuals or businesses. Subsidies for business include payments to agriculture and nationalized industries struggling to survive in a highly competitive national and international industry; for example, services such as railway services are subsidised by governments. In this context, the government may give subsidies to businesses such as farms so that they can sell their product at lower prices but still achieve a financial gain.

3. Subsidies for Individuals

Subsidies for individuals include transfer payments such as housing benefits, which helps low-income families with their rent, and community and public facilities such as libraries and leisure centres. Moreover, subsidies for individuals include student grants and payments to independent schools, as well as national insurance benefits—especially state retirement pensions, unemployment benefits, child benefits, and sickness benefits.

Based on government revenue sources and government sector expenditures, if government expenditures exceed the government's income, the government is in financial deficit; contrarily it has a financial surplus when income exceeds expenditures. In this way, a government's revenue deficit or surplus equals its income minus government expenditures. Government deficit can result from:

a. Tax cuts on income
b. Tax cuts on government expenditures
c. Increase in expenditure on goods and services

    d.   Increase in subsidies for business

    e.   Increase in subsidies for individuals

A reduction of government deficit would result from decreasing government expenditures and privatizing nationalized industries.

Moreover, total government expenditures are expressed as a percentage of gross domestic product, which explains that a fall in total expenditures would also cause a government financial deficit. At this point, government deficit reduction would result from an increase in GDP.

Furthermore, government deficit could result from a tax rate increase in businesses' or individuals' income, which in turn causes a fall in consumption and investments. In this regard, a reduction in government deficit would result from a decrease in income tax rates and an increase in the value-added taxes—as well as a raise of taxes on the wealthiest taxpayers, or an increase in money supply, or a rise in the expenditures of goods and services.

When tax rates increase on income, it causes business revenue to fall—and in turn there is a fall in business revenue, which causes government revenue to falls. These factors mean that the fall of revenue is caused by a fall in the scale of activity as result of an increase in income tax rates. For example, a tax rate increase in fuel causes an increase in fuel prices; consequently, people stop driving cars, and others sell big cars and buy small cars, which causes a decline in oil sales.

In relation to the reduction of the Irish budget deficit, the Irish economy needs tax cuts on small- and medium-sized enterprises, and on low-income taxpayers. It also needs a fair raise in the taxes of the wealthiest taxpayers. The country would benefit from more privatization of some Irish nationalized industries or public services.

In the beginning of the Irish financial crisis, Irish banks did not have enough capital, which means that they did not have enough reserves. So if Eurozone policymakers chose a facilitation to lend to Irish private banks instead of a loan to the Irish government, the money could cause the Irish economy to have a fast recovery. The direction taken by the Irish government to reduce government deficit was and is in the wrong direction, because if the government keeps running up deficits, it will increase Irish debt and interest payments. Therefore the increase in Irish debts will cause problems in the government's borrowing requirements.

6. How Can Eurozone Governments Influence Sustainable Job Creation?

Since 2008, Eurozone governments have responded to a Eurozone economic crisis mainly by a policy of reducing government budget deficit instead of by a policy of restoring businesses' confidence. Thus Eurozone governments raised tax rates on incomes and indirect taxes on businesses while cutting taxpayers' income. In this context, many still want to know if this policy is not the opposite of job creation. Before responding to this question, it is necessary to know whether the governments believe that private businesses create more jobs than the governments' institutions. If private sectors could create more jobs than public sectors, then private sectors would need to have more support from governments; this means that public sectors—particularly government welfare sectors—would gain less funding.

In my opinion, I believe that more support from government is needed in the private sectors, because the private sectors employ more employees than the public sectors. Since the 2008 economic crisis, unemployment continues to increase in the Eurozone countries because many private sectors have closed down. Moreover, as many private sectors continue to close down, youth unemployment and the university graduate unemployment continues to be at a high level, because private sectors employ more young employees than public sectors. Additionally, there is more youth unemployment because private sectors, which employ more semi-skilled employees, have closed down. These are the facts that indicate why the private sectors create more jobs than the public sectors. Eurozone governments can influence job creation by investing more in the private sector services while supporting businesses. Unemployment can only slow down when goods and services of the private sectors are increasingly consumed. If goods and services of private sectors are increasingly consumed, then private sectors are hiring more employees, and unemployment will decrease.

To answer the question whether the governments believe more employment in the private sectors, I believe that they don't. They do not believe that more jobs must be created in private sectors because since 2008, government efforts have not been directed to the private sector. As explained in the text of this book, instead the Eurozone governments' efforts are directed to reduce the budget deficit. Although some would agree that Eurozone governments have no other alternatives to reduce the deficit, the Eurozone governments have responded to the economic crisis in the direction opposite to how more jobs can be created, in order to reduce deficit in the EU areas.

Governments create an environment for more jobs when they invests more in the private sectors. In other words, governments can create more jobs if their investments are more directed in the businesses. In contrast, even though public services create jobs, the goal of public sectors is to supply services to the public and private sectors. Public services do not compete between them, because their work is designed for no profits. Thus while private goods and services are profit-driven, public goods and services are not driven by profits. In this context, therefore, public services are not capable of creating more jobs because of a lack of competitiveness in their services. Competition increases profit from the services, and more profits increases job creation.

Private sectors are unable to create more jobs when the goods and services they supply to the public and government agencies are not consumed. In other words, when consumers have no purchasing power to buy goods and services produced by private sectors, the result is no job creation in the private sectors.

In summary, private sectors, and particularly businesses, create more jobs because their goals are to work hard for both profits and to stay in business. Moreover, they are more innovative. They do cost reduction on their goods and services while creating new goods and services. By contrast, public sector services create less jobs, and their goals is to supply services to the public and private sectors. With the exception of education services, public services often do not efficiently provide services because they do not work for profits; thus their services are less innovative, whereas private services are more innovative. More investment from the government is needed in the private sector than in the public sector, because the private sector employs more workers than the public sector.

Though this book discusses political party ideology in relation to job creation, it recognizes that their differences are embodied in the taxation system and regulation. Social democrats and political parties including the so-called left-wing parties prefer an increase in taxation and regulation, whereas conservatives, the so called right wing political parties, prefer deregulation and a decrease in taxation, particularly in business. The book recognizes the weaknesses and strengths of all political parties in relation to sustainable job creation. Their weaknesses and strengths are founded in their affiliate ideology of taxation and regulation.

The book recognizes the necessity of restructuring institutions of the Eurozone economic integration. The primary goal of Eurozone and European Union is for strong economic integration in the European Union, so the European Union need tougher regulation rules, particularly for integrating EU economies. Otherwise the EU economy will continue in the wrong direction.

CHAPTER VI

▼

Saving the US Economy

1. New Ways for Saving the US Economy after the New York Market Crash in 1929

Despite that the saying "Planning is a dirty word in America", after the New York Market Crash in 1929, private individuals and government officials at all levels—including states and cities—advocated planning.[13] The popularity of planning indicates a sense that the past ways of doing things are no longer adequate and that some new ways have to be found for saving the US economy. As for those new ways for saving the US economy, in 1933 a National Resources Committee inspected national resources and advised the government on their use on a permanent basis. In 1939, the committee was turned into the National Resources Planning Board, which Franklin Roosevelt referred to as "the planning arm of my executive office, charged with preparation of long-range plans for the development".[14] The planning board generated a substantial amount of research and thinking on the structure of the American economy, particularly on manpower, public works, the location of industry, consumer behaviour, and waterpower. It brought together representatives of many Washington agencies and also did much work through committees that drew in businessmen and other private groups, as well as many leading economists contributed.

---

[13] See Pinder J. (1982), *National Industrial Strategies and the World Economy*, An Atlantic Institute for International Affairs Research Volume, Croom Helm, London, p. 166.

[14] See NRPB, *National Resources Development;* Report for 1942, letter of transmittal to Congress.

The committee considered more measures, including a plan to rebuild the merchant marine, revive shipbuilding by subsidies, and protect legislation. It also included the separation of commercial banks from investment banking by the Glass-Steagall Act, and the creation of the Securities and Exchange Commission with initial regulatory powers, which have over time done much to shape the structure of the industry. These efforts have had lasting effects and are among the elements that make the American economy of the twentieth century so different from that of the country's first 150 years.[15] Of the many ways to help businesses in difficulty, one of the most important was the provision of capital through the Reconstruction Finance Corporation (RFC). The RFC was created by President Hoover and was expanded by President Roosevelt. The RFC provided loans, and although it was considered an instrument of industry policy, its help was directed to all kinds of firms.

The Trade Agreements Act of 1934 also played an important role in stimulating the US economy. Even though the aim of the Trade Agreements Act was the expansion of American exports, its secondary aim was the reduction of American tariffs by reciprocal bargaining. The reduction of tariffs was selective both to preserve bargaining strength and to avoid loss to American domestic interests. In this regard, during the London Economic Conference in 1933, the American delegation rejected the short-term stabilization of exchange rates. The export effect was assumed to be strongest in certain sectors, such as automobiles, electrical equipment, consumer durables, and agriculture. The Trade Agreements Act inaugurated the longest period in American history in which tariffs were lowered. In this respect, the reduction of American import barriers and the expansion of American direct investment abroad brought about considerable changes in the structure of the American economy.

The aim of the presidency of Franklin Roosevelt was to stimulate recovery and sustain employment; however, reforms were also major objectives. There were a number of measures with structural purposes,

---

[15]   See Pinder J. (1982) *National Industrial Strategies and the World Economy*, p168.

and many had structural effects, particularly in the long term. There was more use of industry measures than had been usual in the American economy.

By the early 1960s, many past measures were under attack. The expansion of production in Europe and Japan increased competition for American industry. The deficit appeared in the United States' balance of payments. The opening of the Common Market in Europe was seen both to provide some opportunities for American trade and investment, and also to put the United States at some disadvantage. The Trade Expansion Act of 1962 envisaged more removal of trade barriers among industrial countries than had been considered before. It also created the government adjustment assistance for labour and business damaged by imports. By the late 1960s, the strains on American economic policies had grown. Many factors contributed, including the deterioration of the balance of payments, the malfunctioning of the international monetary system, inadequate measures of monetary reform, the apparent loss of the competitiveness of parts of American industry, stagflation, disturbances connected with the Vietnam War, the common American belief that Europe and Japan were not carrying their fair share of the burdens of defending and managing the free world, and American labour's increased resistance to import competition combined with the belief that the large volume of direct investment abroad by American companies resulted in the export of jobs.

The extensive reduction of tariffs emphasised the importance of nontariff barriers and trade-distorting practices, which were often deeply rooted in domestic economic strategies. A common American view, particularly in business, was that Japan and Europe made extensive use of these instruments while the American market was wide open to competition. All these factors contributed to the explosion of economic nationalism reflected in the unilateral actions of the Nixon administration, which disengaged the dollar from gold and temporarily established new barriers to international trade.

By the 1970s the US economy was in a difficult spot because the price of oil had risen dramatically and caused high inflation rates, which triggered a recession in the US economy. In the 1960s and 1970s, the Chrysler Corporation had a history of financial instability, and in 1979 Chrysler's total loss for the year was $1.12 billion.[16] Ford and General Motors also experienced large losses in 1979 and 1980 as a consequence of the sharp rise in the price of gasoline and the worst economic downturn since the Great Depression. "In 1980, General Motors, Ford and Chrysler lost a record $ 4.2 billion as their sales in that year plummeted 30 per cent below 1978 sales, reaching their lowest level since 1961."[17] As unemployment and other problems of recession increased, along with import competition, the threat of failure of great enterprises and the worry about the balance of trade and the state of the dollar made the American government intervene in the economy. In this context, the US automobile industry received federal loan guarantees to avoid bankruptcy. In 1980, the Chrysler Corporation Loan Guarantee Act of 1979 was signed into law as PL 96-185. With the exception of the 1990s American economic boom, the American economy is still unstable. Despite that, government intervention in economy is considered by many Americans as a weak economic strategy. In early 2008, President Bush signed a $700 billion emergency bailout for the banking industry to deal with their financial crises. Moreover, President Obama signed a General Motors (GM) bailout. As a result, the American economy started recovering at the end of 2011. This is evidence that early government intervention is imperative for rescuing the economy when it is in financial failure.

---

[16] See US General Accounting Office, *Guidelines for Rescuing Large Failing Firms and Municipalities,* GAO Report GGD-84-34, March 29, 1984, p. 15.

[17] See Stephen D. Cohen, *The Route to Japan's Voluntary Export Restraints on Automobiles,* Working Paper No 20, School of International Service, American University, p. 2, available at http://www.gwu.edu/~nsarchiv/japan/scohenwp.htm, visited December 1, 2011.

2. The US Presidents' Economic Policies from 1929 to 2008

President Herbert Hoover, 1929-1933

As a member of the Republican Party, during Hoover's presidency, his plan was to reform the regulatory system, believing that a federal bureaucracy should have limited regulation over the US economic system. In this context, he considered his presidency a vehicle for improving the conditions of all Americans by encouraging public and private cooperation. Hoover saw volunteerism as preferable to government intervention. Thus instead of the government aiding the poor, he preferred to encourage churches and social institutions to aid Americans unable to sell their labour. In 1929, Hoover's treasury secretary, Andrew Mellon, enacted tax cuts which cut tax rates on personal income. Therefore when the Great Depression began in 1929, government revenues dropped dramatically. As a result, in 1932 Mellon asked Congress to consider a tax increase, and Congress passed the Revenue Act to reduce government deficit. The act increased taxes on the highest income earners and also increased excise taxes.

In his presidency, Hoover expanded the civil service of federal positions, and he cancelled private oil leases on government lands. He also instructed the Justice Department and the Internal Revenue Service to pursue tax evasion. He proposed an act for tax reduction on low income, but it was not enacted. Although he closed certain tax loopholes for the wealth, Hoover doubled the number of hospital facilities to veterans. He wrote a children's charter that advocated the protection of every child regardless of a race or gender. Hoover proposed an act on federal loans for urban slum clearances, but it was not passed. He created an anti-trust division in the Justice Department. While he organised the Federal Bureau of Prisons, he instituted prison reforms and reorganised the Bureau of Indian Affairs. He proposed a Federal Department of Education but did not get approval. He chaired White House meetings on child health and homebuilding, and he began construction of the Boulder Dam, later named the Hoover Dam. Hoover also signed the Norris-LaGuardia Act (47 Stat. 70), which limited judicial intervention in labour disputes.

Hoover feared that too much government intervention in businesses would destroy individuality and self-reliance, but the big picture of his ideas was to support public-private cooperation as the way to achieve long-term growth. He considered self-reliance to be important to American values. In this way, Hoover believed that African Americans and other races could improve their self-sufficiency with education.

After the 1929 stock market crash, President Hoover rejected government intervention. He believed that the economy would fix itself and argued that government assistance to individuals would reduce their incentive to work. Moreover, he believed that in a period of recession, the government should adopt austerity measures—that is, reduce government expenditures and increase taxes. During the recession he was unwilling to fund welfare programs.

In June 1930, President Hoover enacted the Smoot-Hawley Tariff Act, which raised the US tariffs against foreign imports in order to protect American businesses. The purpose of the Hawley Act was to increase the cost of imported goods, encouraging Americans to buy goods made in America in order to raise revenue for the government. In 1931, he insisted that major banks in the country form an association known as the National Credit Corporation. He encouraged the NCC to loan to banks in order to prevent them bankruptcies.

In 1932, the Hoover administration enacted an Emergency Relief and Construction Act, which authorized funds for public works programs and the creation of the Reconstruction Finance Corporation (RFC). The RFC's goal was to provide loans to banks, financial institutions, and business corporations, as well as railroads and farmers.

President Hoover believed that Democrats were against every measure he offered to the Congress to restore economy. Under Hoover's presidency, government debts climbed from 20 per cent to 40 per cent.[18]

---

[18] Historical Statistics, United States series (1976), F32 and Y493.

President Franklin D. Roosevelt, 1933-1945

President Franklin Delano Roosevelt was inaugurated on March 4, 1933. During this period, the United States was experiencing deep recession, the Great Depression. At this time, prices, employment, and industry production fell; the US economy was in decline, and many banks were bankrupt. As a member of the American Democratic Party, President Roosevelt attributed the Great Depression to financial institutions such as banks. During his first hundred days as president, he initiated the New Deal Programs; amongst these was preparation of recovery legislation that set up the Agricultural Adjustment Administration (AAA) to support farm prices. Congress passed this legislation.

The AAA was to purchase farms' overproduction in order to decrease farm prices. Moreover, Congress passed legislation which set up the Civilian Conservation Corps (CCC) to hire unemployed young men to work on rural local projects. In order to finance railroads and industry, President Roosevelt expanded the Hoover Reconstruction Finance Corporation. To instigate American banks' confidence, he signed the Glass-Steagall Act, which created the Federal Deposit Insurance Corporation (FDIC).

In addition, Congress passed the 1933 National Industrial Recovery Act (NIRA), which was to encourage the industry sectors' removal of unfair competitive practices and to promote productive activities by utilising the resources available; the act was also to improve the standard of labour while reducing unemployment. With Republican Senator George Norris, Roosevelt created the Tennessee Valley Authority (TVA), a state-owned industrial enterprise. Additionally, the main legislations of banking regulations were passed in 1934, and Roosevelt helped create the Securities and Exchange Commission to regulate Wall Street. In order to fight deflation, Roosevelt declared Executive Order 6102 requiring gold coin, gold bullion, and certificates to be delivered to the government, and its prices were increased.

In his second term, he introduced the second New Deal Programs. These programs were intended to end the Great Depression by raising expenditures. The program introduced many legislations, including the Works Progress Administration (WPA) in 1935. The WPA hired workers to build roads, new hospitals, city halls, courthouses, and schools.

Additionally, Congress passed the Social Security Act, which established social security to the elderly, the sick, and the poor. In 1935 Congress passed the Wagner Act, (later the National Labour Relations Act) to establish the right of workers to organise unions while engaging in collective bargaining. President Roosevelt also issued Executive Order 9250, which increased tax rates for incomes exceeding twenty-five thousand dollars. Under Roosevelt, government deficit was not reduced.

According to Stanley Lebergott, between 1929 and 1933, the unemployment rate increased by over 20 per cent,[19] but under President Roosevelt, the rate of unemployment dropped to 6 per cent between 1933 and 1941 (Darby 1976).[20]

---

[19] See Margo R. A. (1993), "Employment and Unemployment in the 1930s", *Journal of Economic Perspectives* 7, no. 2, p. 41-59.

[20] See Steindl F. G. (2007), *Understanding Economic Recovery in the 1930s*, Endogenous Propagation in the Great Depression.

President Harry S. Truman, 1945-1953

A member of the Democratic Party, President Truman was a supporter of Roosevelt's programs. In his second term, he implemented the Marshall Plan, an economic policy which was planned to rebuild Europe after the Second World War. President Truman established new economic strategies, including the Council of Economic Advisers (CEA) and the Joint Economic Committee of the Congress (JEC). These structures were established by the Employment Act of 1946, which was aimed at increasing unemployment. In 1947 he supported initiatives such as housing for the poor and federal assistance to education. He vetoed tax bills to raise tariffs on imported wool and a bill to reduce income taxes. Because of the continuation of an increase in the prices of food in 1947 and 1948, he asked for a return to price controls, but Congress rejected this suggestion. In 1949 he announced policies he called "Fail Deal", which included an increase in the minimum wage, expansion of the social security programme, a housing bill, and a national health insurance. Congress did not approve all parts of the Fail Deal, but it passed the public housing bill and the clearance bill. In the same year Congress supported an increase in the minimum wage and social security in 1950. Even though President Truman's economic strategy sought to balance the federal government budget through a combination of high taxes and limited expenditures, in 1949 he abandoned this policy and gave tax breaks to businesses. As result, in 1950 the US economy started perking up—though it was depressed by the Korean War. In this period, Congress passed the Defence Production Act, which gave more power to the government to control the US economic activities, including control of consumers and real estate credits, wages and price stabilisation, and labour disputes. Moreover, President Truman issued an executive order to create the Office of Defence Mobilisation.

President Dwight D. Eisenhower, 1953-1961

President Eisenhower was a member of the Republican Party. Eisenhower's economic policy focused on stability and balancing the budget, and he also maintained Roosevelt's economic strategies and legislation, including social security. Under his presidency, America created the National Aeronautics and Space Administration (NASA). President Eisenhower stimulated the American economy by government spending in construction. He signed the Federal Aid Highway Act in 1956, which authorised the construction of new highways that linked the nation. In his presidency, economic activity perked up from 1953 to 1954. The American economy rose strongly until the end of 1956, when it slowed down in the latter part of 1957. The American economy rose again after 1959 as result of a rise in sales, and it strongly recovered in the second half of 1961.

President John F. Kennedy, 1961-1963

Among his presidential acts, Kennedy issued an order in 1961 establishing the Peace Corps. Congress approved the Peace Corps as a permanent agency within the State Department, and Kennedy signed the legislation on September 22, 1961. The Peace Corps is dedicated to assisting other countries in their development. President Kennedy continued Roosevelt's legacy: He signed legislation raising the minimum wage and social security benefits. He funded research related to mental illness, and he allocated funds in the slum areas. President Kennedy referred to his economic policies as the "New Frontier". His goal was to set up a program for funding education, medical care for the elderly, and government intervention for economic recovery. His requests for funding elementary and secondary schools and for Medicare plan to provide health insurance to the elderly were also denied.

In 1963, President Kennedy proposed a tax reform that included tax cuts, and Congress passed it in 1964. During his presidency, the American economy turned towards good health. Inflation was low and unemployment was lessened; both industry production and sales rose.

President Lyndon B. Johnson, 1963-1969

A member of the Democratic Party, President Lyndon enacted the Civil Rights Act of 1964, aimed to ban discrimination based on a race and gender in the working environment and to end segregation in all public facilities. Moreover, he signed the Economic Opportunity Act of 1964, which was designed to eradicate American poverty. In the same year, President Lyndon signed the Elementary and Secondary Education Act (ESEA) to provide funds to both public and private schools, and these funds were aimed to help struggling communities while fighting illiteracy. He also signed the Immigration and Nationality Act of 1965, which President Kennedy had initiated. Moreover, he set up the National Endowment for the Humanities and the National Endowment for the Arts, to support artists and humanists. He also signed the Public Broadcasting Act to create educational television programs and to supplement the broadcast networks. In 1965, he signed Medicare and Medicaid acts. The Medicare program was created to facilitate medical services to the elderly and Americans with low income. The Medicare program still exists and is sponsored by the government through the Medicaid program.

President Richard Nixon, 1969-1974

A member of Republican Party, Nixon became president when the rates of inflation and unemployment were climbing. His economic strategies were centred around tackling these issues. As described in the 1972 Annual Report of the Council of Economic Advisers,

> The United States suspended the convertibility of the dollar into gold or other reserve assets, for the first time since 1934. It imposed a temporary surcharge, generally at the rate of 10 per cent, on dutiable imports. Prices, wages and rents were frozen for 90 days, to be followed by a more flexible and durable—but still temporary—system of mandatory controls.

In August 1971, President Nixon introduced a ninety-day wage and price freeze and set up the Price Commission and Cost of Living Council. Under Nixon, America created the Occupational Safety and Health Administration Act (OSHA), the Clean Air Act of 1970, the Pesticide Control Act (1972), and the Clean Water Act. Although President Nixon was aware of the importance of NASA, he was unwilling to maintain its funding.

President Gerald Ford, 1974-1977

President Ford was a member of the Republican Party, and he became president when Nixon resigned on August 8, 1974. During his presidency, the rates of inflation and unemployment were rising. In October 1974, he proposed a rise in the tax rates and a reduction in federal expenditures. However, because of economic slowdown instead of recovery, in January 1975 Ford introduced tax cuts to stimulate the economy. In March 1975, Congress passed tax cuts but increased expenditures on government programs. Moreover, Congress passed the Revenue Adjustment Act of 1975, which extended the provisions of tax cuts. In the Omnibus Energy Bill, President Ford accepted a 12 per cent reduction in domestic oil prices in return for the authority to end price controls on oil over forty-month period. Under his presidency, Congress passed an act in 1975 which allowed education for all handicapped. By 1976, the US economy started to recover.

President Jimmy Carter, 1977-1981

A member of the Democratic Party, President Carter took office when the US economy was still recovering from inflation and high unemployment. His ambition was to reduce unemployment and balance the budget. In relation to high unemployment rates, he proposed a reduction on both personal and business taxes while raising government expenditures in the public sector and in job-training programs.[21] His proposition was rejected, but another fiscal stimulus that included some minor tax reductions and employment programs was passed.[22] Moreover, Carter implemented a program of "voluntary wage and price standard"; the goal of this program was to reduce the inflation rate by creating an environment that encouraged cooperation with pay and price standards. Thus he requested cooperation between employers and employees for

---

[21] See Economic Report of the President, 1977, Washington DC: Unites States Printing Office, 1977, p. 31-32.

[22] See Economic Report of the President, 1978, p. 51-52.

reducing wages, as well as businesses to reduce prices.[23] In August 1980, President Carter announced his Economic Renewal Program, which attempted to stimulate the economy through a partnership between the private and the government sectors. This policy allowed the government to lower corporate taxes to stimulate investment and adjustments to the income tax structure.[24]

Under his presidency, Carter signed the Chrysler Corporation Loan Guarantee Act of 1979, the aim of which was to recover the American automobile industry from financial problems. Additionally, he signed the Airline Deregulation Act to eliminate certain governmental controls from the commercial aviation industry and to open it up to competition and new opportunities for emerging airlines. Furthermore, Carter encouraged energy conservation and installed solar water-heating panels on the White House.

---

[23] See Stephen Woolck (1984), "The Economic Policies of the Carter Administration", in *The Carter Year: The President and Policy Making*, M. Glenn Abernathy, Dilys M. Hill, and Phil Williams, eds., Frances Printer, London.

[24] See Public papers of the Presidents, Jimmy Carter, 1980-81, Vol. II, Washington DC, 1982, p. 1585-91

President Ronald Reagan, 1981-1989

To stimulate the US economy, President Reagan proposed tax cuts and signed the Economic Recovery Tax Act of 1981, which was designed to encourage saving by increasing returns through low taxation on property income and by increasing investment through various tax incentives. Moreover, in 1982 he signed into law the Job Training Partnerships Act of 1982, which was designed to train unemployed and to improve employment status. President Reagan also signed the Tax Reform Act of 1986, which is referred to as the second of two Reagan tax cuts and lowered personal and corporate income tax rates. The act mandated that capital gains would be taxed at the same rate as ordinary income, and though it eliminated the investment tax credits, it extended the

Research and Development Tax Credit. President Reagan also signed the Tax Equity and Fiscal Responsibility Act of 1982, which raised taxes an average of forty-seven billion dollars in each of the four years after it was enacted.[25]

Reagan's economic strategy of low taxation did not reduce US deficit—there were increases in the federal debt and annual deficit. Between the beginning and the end of his presidency, the annual deficit almost tripled: gross national debt increased from $995 billion to $2.9 trillion.[26]

In relation to deficit reduction, he signed the Deficit Reduction Act of 1984. Strategies used to reduce government deficit included a cut in government expenditures to Federal education programs, the Environment Protection Agency, Medicaid, and food stamps, as well as a reduction to Aid to Families with Dependent Children (AFDC). Furthermore, President Regan's economic policies also included freezing the minimum wage at $3.35 per hour.

---

[25] See Thorndike, J. (2011), "Why Reagan Raised Taxes and We Should, Too", *Echoes* [online], available at http://www.bloomberg.com/news/2011-08-16/why-reagan-raised-taxes-and-we-should-too-echoes.html, accessed February 15, 2012.

[26] See Magazzino, M. (2012), "The Economic Policy of Ronald Reagan: Between Supply-Side and Keynesianism", *European Journal of Social Sciences* 27, no. 3, p. 319-334.

President George H. W. Bush, 1989-1993

A member of the Republican Party, President Bush was the successor to President Reagan. His ambition was to reduce the US deficit spawned by the Reagan presidency. Despite the fact that in his election campaign he promised not to raise taxes, he accepted the Democrats' proposition for raising taxes. He also increased government expenditures and signed a bill providing additional benefits for unemployed. Additionally, he was a supporter of both developing technology research and increasing federal expenditures for education and childcare. In his presidency he promoted educational reform, home ownership, and environment protection. He also signed the Americans with Disabilities Act; the Clean Air Act Amendment, which required cleaner burning fuels; and the Immigration Act of 1990, which increased legal immigration to the United States.

President Bill Clinton, 1993-2001

A member of Democratic Party, President Clinton was inaugurated as the forty-second president of the United States on January 20, 1993. In order to reduce the US deficit, he signed the Omnibus Budget Reconciliation Act of 1993, which increased taxes on income of some wealthy individuals and corporations, while cutting some government spending. Another act President Clinton signed was the Family and Medical Leave Act of 1993, which allowed employees to take unpaid leave for a serious medical condition or pregnancy. In 1994 Clinton signed into law the North American Free Trade Agreement. In 1994, his administration launched the first official White House website. For making accessible information from federal agencies to the public, Bill Clinton issued an executive order requesting the heads of all federal agencies to use information technology. Moreover, in 1996 he signed the Illegal Immigration Reform and Immigration Responsibility Act, which focuses on illegal immigration reform and includes some measures against illegal immigration, including border patrol and enforcement.

President George W. Bush, 2001-2009

A member of Republican Party, President George W. Bush signed the No Child Left Behind Act, which was designed to improve the performance of America's elementary schools. Bush increased funding in the National Institute of Health, and he created programs to strengthen education in sciences and mathematics for American high school students. Like President Reagan, President Bush used tax cuts to stimulate the US economy. His tax cuts lowered federal income tax rates and capital gains tax rates, as well as the tax rate on dividend income; it also increased the child tax credit. He signed the Medicare Act of 2003, a designed Medicare reform that includes prescription drug benefits, and an executive order to tackle environmental issues. Bush vetoed Children's health insurance legislation. Furthermore, in 2006 he reduced funding for the National Institute of Health. Under his presidency, he also increased government expenditures. During the 2008 economic crisis, he signed a $700 billion emergency bailout for the banking industry to deal with the crisis. Due to increases in US military expenditures abroad and the bailout, the US debt and deficit rose dramatically.

3. How the United States Reduced Its Deficits in the 1960s

It is possible that some American politicians may think that the US federal government can reduce the deficit. In 1956-1957, the United States experienced deficits as a consequence of serving or enabling other countries to rebuild their monetary reserves. The US deficits of this period were regarded as a result of some competitive inadequacy, especially in view of discrimination against imports.[27] Moreover, between 1958 and 1959, the United States experienced deficit which originated from US exports that fell because of a change in the world's economy. The fall in US exports was particularly severe from mid-1957 to mid-1958, and in the following years. At this time, a decline in production in the United States was also evident. After 1959, the deficits were reduced; however, it remained at a high level because of the increase in the foreign gold and liquid dollar holdings through transactions with the United States. The increase recorded outflow of United States private, short-term capital and recorded transfers equalling $3.9 billion in 1960 and $2.5 billion in 1961.[28] During 1962 its deficit was significantly reduced. In addition to the rise of US exports, the deficit was significantly reduced by a high level of business activity in America.[29] This means that a practical way to facilitate reduction in the US deficit may depend on the maintenance of a high rate of business activity in America, and an especially high rate of business activity in the American foreign trade partners. In other words, American economic growth depends particularly on the high rate of American exports as result of expansion of foreign businesses who import American goods and services. This means that the United States' foreign policy in relation to free trade is a key for its economic growth. Thus American domestic demand is not enough to sustain and stimulate American economy.

---

[27] See Hal B. Lary (1963), *Problems of the United States as World Trader and Banker*, National Bureau of Economic Research, p. 19.

[28] See Hal B. Lary (1963), *Problems of the United States as World Trader and Banker*, National Bureau of Economic Research, p. 37.

[29] See Hal B.Lary (1963), *Problems of the United States as World Trader and Banker*, National Bureau of Economic Research, p. 40.

CONCLUSIONS

▼

How to Create and Sustain Growth

Goods and Services	Employment	Unemployment	Government Revenues	Growth
Increase goods and services	Increase	Decrease	Increase	Increase
Decrease goods and services	Decrease	Increase	Decrease	Decline
Increase profits in businesses	Increase	Decrease	Increase	Increase
Tax rises in businesses	Decrease	Increase	Decrease	Decline
Low tax in business	Increase	Decrease	Decrease	Tends to Decline
Tax rise in public sectors	Decrease	Increase	Decrease	Decline
Low tax in public sectors	Increase	Decrease	Decrease	Tends to Decline
Increase income	Increase	Decrease	Increase	Tends to Decline
Decrease income	Increase	Decrease	Decrease	Tends to Decline
Increase government spending	Increase	Decrease	Decrease	Increase
Austerity	Decrease	Increase	Decrease	Decline

Fiscal consolidation[30]	Decrease	Increase	Decrease	Decline
Education	Sustain	Decrease	Sustain	Sustain
R&D[31] and innovation	Sustain	Decrease	Sustain	Sustain
Good governance	Sustain	Decrease	Sustain	Sustain
Bad governance	Decrease	Increase	Decrease	Decline

---

[30]   Government saving while spending.
[31]   Research and development.

SELECTED BIBLIOGRAPHY

▼

Connelly O. (2000), *The French Revolution and Napoleonic Era*, Third Edition, Belmont, CA: Thomson Wadsworth.

Cohen, S. D. (1981), "The Route to Japan's Voluntary Export Restraints on Automobiles: An Analysis of the U.S. Government's Decision Making Process", Working Paper No. 20, School of International Service and American University.

Comptroller, G. (1984), Report to the Congress of the United States: *Guidelines for Rescuing Large Failing Firms and Municipalities*, GAO/GGD 84-34, p. 15.

Denison, E. (1962), "The Sources of Economic Growth in the United States", *American Economic Review* 52, no. 4, p. 123-128.

Denison, E. (1962), *The Sources of Economic Growth in the United States and the Alternatives Before Us*, New York: Committee on Economic Development.

El-Agraa, A. M. (2007), *The European Union: Economics and Policies*, Eight Edition, Cambridge University Press, p. 109-129.

Heywood, A. (2003). *Political Ideologies: An Introduction*, Third Edition, Palgrave Macmillan.

Kennedy, J. V. (1993), "The Omnibus Budget Reconciliation Act of 1993: Will It Reduce The Deficit?" *MAPI Policy Review*, Washington DC, 20036, PR-125.

Keynes, J. M. (1936), *The General Theory of Employment, Interest and Money.* Online at http: //www.marxists.org/reference/subject/economics/Keynes/general-theory.

Kletzner, L. (2002), *Imports, Exports and Jobs: What Does Trade Mean for Employment and Job Loss?* W. E. Upjohn Institute for Employment Research.

Lary, H. B. (1963), *Problems of the United States as World Trader and Banker,* Woodhaven Press Associates Corp.

Laffer, A. B., *Supply-Side Economics,* Encyclopaedia Britannica. Online at http://www.britannica.com/EBchecked/topic/574677/supply-side-economics.

Mankiw, N. G. and Taylor, M. P. (2008), *Macroeconomics: Inflation and Unemployment in the United Kingdom,* Worth Publishers, p. 402.

Margo, R. A. (1993), "Employment and Unemployment in the 1930s", *The Journal of Economic Perspectives* 7, no. 2, p. 41-59.

Magazzino, C. (2012), "The Economic Policy of Ronald Reagan: Between Supply-Side and Keynesianism", *European Journal of Sciences* 27, no. 3, p. 319-334.

Organisation for Economic Co-operation and Development (2009), *The Jobs Crisis: What Are the Implications for Employment and Social Policy?* OECD Employment Outlook.

Parkin, M. and King, D. (1992), *Economics,* Addison-Wesley Publishing Company Inc.

Pinder, J. (1982), *National Industrial Strategies and the World Economy,* Allanheld, Osmun Publishers.

Smith, A. (1776) *An Inquiry into the Nature and Causes of the Wealth of Nations.* Online at http://www.marxists.org/reference/archive/smith-adam/works/wealth-of-nations.

Steindl F. G. (2007), *Understanding Economic Recovery in the 1930s: Endogenous Propagation in the Great Depression*, University of Michigan Press.

Spaak P. H. (1956), Intergovernmental Committee on European Integration: The Brussels Report on the General Common Market, AEI.

Todaro, M. P. (1997), *Economic Development*, Fifth Edition, Longman.

Internet Sources

Reports & Studies: http://www.socialsecurity.gov/history/reports/NRPB/NRPBreport.html

William J. Clinton Presidential Library: http://www.clintonlibrary.gov

Eisenhower Presidential Library and Museum: http://www.eisenhower.archives.gov

Franklin D. Roosevelt Presidential Library and Museum: http://www.fdrlibrary.marist.edu

Gerald R. Ford Museum: http://www.fordlibrarymuseum.gov/default.asp

George W. Bush Presidential Library and Museum: http://www.georgewbushlibrary.smu.edu

Herbert Hoover Presidential Library and Museum: http://www.hoover.archives.gov

John F. Kennedy Presidential Library and Museum: http://www.jfklibrary.org

Jimmy Carter Library and Museum: http://www.jimmycarterlibrary.gov

LBJ Presidential Library: http://www.lbjlibrary.org

Nixon Presidential Library and Museum: http://www.nixonlibrary.gov

Ronal Reagan Presidential Foundation and Library: http://www.reaganfoundation.org

Harry S. Truman Library and Museum: http://www.trumanlibrary.org

The White House: http://www.whitehouse.gov

ABOUT THE AUTHOR

▼

André Hakizimana, BA, MA (economics), is a reader in the Irish economy and a reader in the strategy of job creation. He has written a number of articles in the business, published by ArticlesBase.com. As a business consultant, he was hired by PM Group Ireland, Science Foundation Ireland, and Bord Gáis Ireland. André recognises that the consequence of a lack of understanding of the origins of economic growth is a country's cyclical economic downturn. He knows that failure is natural, not a problem, and he argues that in addition to economic strategy, governments need to include strategies that lessen the effect of recession. He lives in Ireland.